CRIMES OF HORROR

BLITZ EDITIONS

Published by Blitz Editions
an imprint of Bookmart Ltd
Registered Number 2372865
Trading as Bookmart Ltd
Desford Road
Enderby
Leicester LE9 5AD

ISBN 1 85605 110 2

This material has previously appeared in *Crimes and Victims*
50 936

Every effort has been made to contact the copyright holders for the pictures.
In some cases they have been untraceable, for which we offer our apologies.
Thanks to the following libraries and picture agencies which supplied pictures:

Associated Press, AP Worldwide, AGIP, Black Museum, Culver Pictures,
Mary Evans Photo Library, Jack Hickes Photography, Fairfax Ltd,
Illustrated London News, Hulton-Deutsch Collection, News Ltd of Australia,
Popperfotos, Press Association, Rex Features, Frank Spooner Pictures,
Syndication International, Suddeutscher Verlag, Topham, UPI/Bettmann

The Author
Frank Smyth began his career as a crime reporter in Yorkshire, and has
since written numerous books on all aspects of crime, including
Detectives in Fact and Fiction, I'm Jack: The Police Hunt for Jack the Ripper and
Cause of Death: A History of Forensic Science.

CRIMES
OF
HORROR

CONSTANZO
Voodoo Murders

In 1989 a Texan student's end-of-term spree 'down Mexico way' ended with his nightmarish execution. He had run into members of a maniacal voodoo cult, as devoted to diabolic ritual as they were to criminal profit

The air of the American southwest is already warm in the middle of March, when the University of Texas at Austin takes its spring break. Students pile into cars and head to the border to revel in the bars of Brownsville, its beach suburb South Padre on the banks of the Rio Grande, and the cantinas of Matamoros, across the Gateway International Bridge in Mexico.

Mark Kilroy, Bill Huddleston, Brent Martin and Bradley Moore drove south on 11 March 1989. Five days later the four friends, all in their twenty-first year, all from the same hometown, Santa Fe near Houston in Texas, were still staggering around the hot spot in a collective euphoric haze.

Above: *Constanzo as a young man in Florida. He was the child of Cuban immigrants who brought their Santeria religion with them.*

Opposite: *Adolfo de Jesus Constanzo, handsome, charismatic and totally evil.*

Left: *Mark Kilroy, a student at the University of Texas. A day trip to Mexico with friends had a horrific ending for him.*

VANISHED

At about two o'clock on the morning of 15 March, the boys joined the crowds of young Americans filtering back up the main street of Matamoros towards the border bridge. Martin and Moore had wandered ahead, and Bill Huddleston paused in an alley to urinate. While doing so he glimpsed Mark Kilroy talking to some Mexicans. When he came out of the alley Mark had vanished.

Rejoining his two friends at the bridge, Bill urged them to hang around in the hope that Mark would join them. When he did not, the trio walked back into Matamoros and searched the bars until dawn. Then they returned to their hotel in South Padre, before filing a missing persons report with the local police.

In fact, Mark Kilroy was in desperate trouble. Like most of his fellow American students, Kilroy shunned the company of the hard, streetwise Mexicans of his own age who drove around Matamoros in their battered pick-

IN HIS DRUNKEN AND TIRED STATE, MARK KILROY WAS UNABLE TO RESIST THE MEXICANS WHO BUNDLED HIM INTO THEIR TRUCK

up trucks. But on the night of his disappearance, Mark was approached by a couple of young Mexicans, who asked him if he wanted a ride.

Slowed by alcohol and fatigue, Kilroy barely had time to reply before he was bundled into a pick-up truck between the two men and driven off down the still busy main street. Kilroy realized that he was in some kind of peril. When the driver got out to relieve himself, he summoned all his wits and ran.

But two other Mexicans were following in a Chevrolet Suburban station wagon. The American was dragged in and driven off once more, this time with a knife at his throat.

The leader of the kidnap team was a twenty-seven-year-old drug smuggler named Serafin Hernandez Garcia, who had turned to the profitable world of crime under the patronage of a Cuban Padrino – 'Godfather' – thirty-seven-year-old Adolfo de Jesus Constanzo.

Constanzo, his underlings believed, was a powerful black magician. He used the spells of Palo Mayombe, the darker side of Santeria, which was the old slave religion of Cuba, to confer on his illegal operations an air of invulnerability from police and rival gangs. He needed a blond-haired, blue-eyed 'Anglo' such as Mark Kilroy as a human sacrifice.

The two battered vehicles drove to a derelict smallholding named the Rancho Santa Elena, about twenty miles south of the border; it was the headquarters of the Constanzo outfit. Kilroy was tied up and bundled into a barn in which the gang stored marijuana. Meanwhile Garcia rang Constanzo, who was at a Brownsville hotel, to say that his sacrifice was ready.

What happened next was described later to the police by David Serna Valdez, one of the kidnappers. Set up inside a shack on the ranch was an altar, on which stood cheap images of Catholic saints, lighted candles, a chalice and seven strips of coloured cloth to represent the seven principal African gods.

LET THE CEREMONY BEGIN

At midday Mark Kilroy was given a meal of bread and scrambled eggs. Then, at two o'clock in the afternoon, he was dragged into the 'temple'. Constanzo was dressed in a white robe, with coloured glass beads around his neck. He was attended by Elio Hernandez Rivera, known in the underground world of drug smugglers as 'Little Elio'. Elio was also known as 'The Executioner' and bore brand marks on his arms, made with the tip of a red hot knife, to mark him for this role. The third man present was Alvaro de Leon Valdez, another of Constanzo's criminal lieutenants.

Mark Kilroy was brought in and forced to kneel over an orange-coloured tarpaulin, while Constanzo lit a cigar. The 'high priest' blew cigar smoke over the bound captive. Next he raised a rum bottle, took a swig and blew the rum out in a fine spray over Mark's head. The victim was thus 'purified'.

Then, as Mark knelt, Constanzo swung a heavy machete and cut off the back of his skull 'with a sound,' David Valdez

Below: *Titled 'La Padrona' (the Godmother) by Constanzo, Sara Maria Aldrete was once a straight-A student in Texas.*

El Coqueto's reaction was to slam his foot on the accelerator and crash his way through, roaring off in his powerful car with the lawmen in hot pursuit.

CAPTURE OF THE UNCATCHABLE

Valdez drove like a demon, but the Federales were dogged in their pursuit and they were helped by the fact that Valdez was high on more than mere drugs. Since the sacrificial ceremony he was convinced, like the rest of the Constanzo gang, that he was under demonic protection and thus invulnerable to arrest and capture. He led the police straight to the Santa Elena ranch.

later recalled, 'like a ripe coconut being split open'.

Constanzo then scooped out the brain and threw it into a cauldron which bubbled over an open fire. The cauldron, already containing a potion of blood, chickens' feet, feathers and a goat's head, was called a *n'ganga* – simply an African cooking pot. For a while, the 'priest' chanted over the sickening stew. Then he encouraged his followers to mutilate Kilroy's body, cutting off facial features, fingers and genitals.

Some three weeks after the terrible events at Santa Elena ranch, David Serna Valdez, who had taken part in the kidnapping of Kilroy and was known as 'El Coqueto' – 'the Flirt' – by his homosexual friends, was driving his Chevrolet Silverado when he came across a police roadblock, manned by members of the Mexican Army and the Federal Judicial Police – the Federales.

Above: *Texas Attorney General Jim Mattox looks down at the blood-stained* **n'ganga** *which contained Mark Kilroy's brain.*

Above right: *The shack at Santa Elena where Mark Kilroy spent his last horrific hours.*

THE BODIES IN THE GRAVES HAD HAD THEIR FINGERS, LIMBS AND GENITALS SEVERED AND THEIR BRAINS SCOOPED FROM THEIR SKULLS

There, Valdez was arrested, and in the ramshackle buildings of the ranch the police found a sizeable reward for their persistence. In addition to large quantities of marijuana and cocaine, they found an arsenal of firearms and ammunition and eleven brand new cars.

Also at the farm was an old caretaker; when the police routinely showed him a photograph of the missing Mark Kilroy, the old man nodded recognition. Yes, he said, the boy had been brought here some weeks ago. The old man had made him a meal of eggs and bread.

A computer search yielded the names and addresses of what appeared to be a large and powerful gang. Within days the police were making arrests. Among others hauled in were Sergio Martinez, known as 'La Mariposa' – 'the Butterfly' – along with Serafin Hernandez Jnr and Elio Hernandez Rivera – Little Elio – who was one of the most prominent names on the Federales' wanted list.

On Tuesday 11 April the Federal Judicial Police took the principal arrested gang members out to the ranch and demanded a guided tour. They found the evil-smelling shack with its breeze-block altar and orange tarpaulin, and noted the paraphernalia of Santeria.

They also found the cast iron *n'ganga* containing the now congealed and decaying lumps of vegetable and animal and human flesh in a soup of black blood.

Eventually thirteen bodies were discovered in nine graves. Mark Kilroy lay three feet under the ground and was identified only through dental records of his lower jaw. Most of the other bodies had been mutilated in a similar fashion to Mark's. Fingers, limbs and genitals were severed, faces obliterated, brains scooped from skulls.

The thirteenth grave was exhumed for the benefit of TV cameras and press photographers. The police made a gang member, Sergio Martinez, do the digging. The grave contained the corpse of a fourteen-year-old whose rib cage had been hacked open. The heart was missing.

With the grim secrets of the Santa Elena ranch laid bare, the police began an intensive search for Adolfo de Jesus Constanzo and his high priestess, Sara Maria Aldrete.

VOODOO CHILD

Constanzo had been born on 1 November 1962 in Miami, Florida, to Delia Gonzales Del Valle and her lover, both of whom had fled Castro's Cuba. Adolfo's father abandoned Delia and the baby soon after the child's birth, and his mother married a Puerto Rican, who brought the boy up as a devout Catholic.

When he was ten, his stepfather died and his mother reverted to old habits to make money. She was the daughter of a priestess of Palo Mayombe back in Cuba, from whom she had learned her craft. Now she began to practise as a magician again, casting spells and charms for the expatriate Cuban community.

As he grew up, his mother taught Adolfo the family magical secrets. But Adolfo also had natural charm and film-star good looks. By the time he was fourteen he had attracted a bevy of women to him.

In 1983, when he was twenty-one, Adolfo moved with his mother to Mexico City, where he became a male model. Soon he was a familiar figure in the city's fashionable circles. As a bisexual, he cultivated links with homosexuals in government and legal circles, and he began to work his way into the lucrative world of drug-dealing. At the same time, according to his mother, he was studying the black arts under a major 'santero' known as 'The Great One', apparently the most powerful magician in Central America. From him, Adolfo learned the use of human sacrifice.

Sara Maria Aldrete had been born in Matamoros on 6 September 1964 and

Above: *Mexican federal policeman, Martin Solozar, examines human remains in one of several shallow graves at the ranch.*

Below: *Police unearth dismembered human remains.*

grew up there. She married at eighteen, divorced at twenty and a year later, in 1985, was accepted into Texas Southernmost College in Brownsville on a two-year physical education course. The tall brunette was extremely attractive and soon caught the attention of Serafin Hernandez Jnr, a smart young man who made his money from the family trade of drug smuggling.

The Hernandez family operated in two 'divisions'. Serafin Snr handled the USA side, until his arrest in February 1987. Serafin Jnr worked out of Matamoros for his young uncle, the feared 'Little Elio' Hernandez Rivera.

Sara Aldrete and Serafin Jnr saw each other at weekends, when Sara came home across the Gateway International Bridge to Matamoros. But one weekend in the autumn of 1986, a Mercedez cut in front of her car, and the handsome Constanzo got out. Using his easy charm instead of the usual Mexican macho approach, Constanzo invited Sara to a café and read her fortune from tarot cards. He told her that someone close to her would come to her with a 'terrible problem'.

Sure enough, two weeks later Serafin Jnr told her how the Hernandez family business was in danger of collapse. Sara was impressed by this demonstration of Constanzo's 'powers', while he saw an opportunity of worming into the confidence of the drugs barons of Mexico City. Soon he was Sara's lover.

Sara was now completely under

Constanzo's spell. During the coming months he took her to his Mexico City home, where he had already begun to dabble in human sacrifice.

SLAUGHTER: A WAY OF LIFE – AND DEATH

In the early part of 1988, acting on Constanzo's instructions, Sara seduced Little Elio. Before long she was convincing him that what he needed was the help of a powerful sorcerer to help him with his family problems. The drugs boss, as superstitious as most of his countrymen, needed little persuasion to meet Constanzo. And, like his nephew and his new mistress, he was instantly impressed.

Constanzo initiated him into the dark rituals of Palo Mayombe, branding him on the shoulders, back and chest with a hot knife to denote his new rank of executioner. Now, Constanzo and Little Elio became joint ceremonial killers, using one of Elio's gang hideouts – the Santa Elena ranch.

Gradually, true to Constanzo's predictions, the Mexican side of the drug business began to improve. Now they needed to place the US side on a solid footing once more. To do this, Constanzo ordered the kidnapping of an 'Anglo' for sacrifice, his white blood being deemed to have better protective powers over Anglo policemen than the Mexican variety. And so Mark Kilroy met his savage end.

No one knows exactly how many ritual

Left: *Martin Quintana was one of Constanzo's many homosexual lovers.*

Below: *Constanzo and Quintana lie together in death after their suicide pact.*

sacrifices were made by Constanzo and his cult, but one informed estimate was that the total was nearer thirty than the thirteen discovered at the ranch. In any case, time was now running out for the black magician and his depraved coterie.

Commandante Benitez Ayala of the Federales led a posse of policemen to Sara's house in Matamoros even before the last of the Santa Elena bodies had been exhumed. Her father showed them her apartment and they burst in. Inside

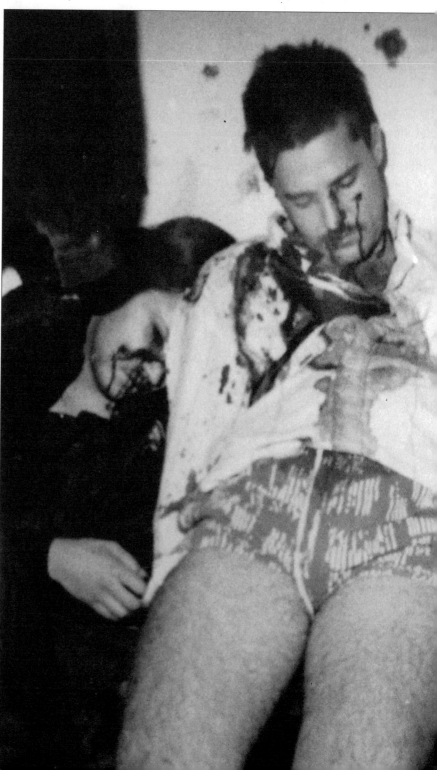

was an altar with candles, blood and bloodstained clothing – but no sign of the sorceress.

That afternoon Commandante Ayala, who himself kept 'white' Santeria charms on his desk at headquarters, summoned a 'curandero' – a Santeria priest. They went out to the ranch, and Ayala called an end to the digging. The curandero sprinkled holy water around the shack which contained the altar and chanted spells. Then he poured petrol over the red tarpaper of the walls, and set fire to the place, burning it to the ground.

As his black magic headquarters burned, Constanzo was on the run with his high priestess. Sara met him at Brownsville, where they boarded an aeroplane for Mexico City. When they arrived there, however, the Federales had already raided his flat, picked up notebooks which named important clients and laid a trap for him.

Constanzo, Sara, Alvaro de Leon Valdez and a number of others collected money at gunpoint from criminal associates, then drove in a convoy to the resort of Cuernavaca, fifty miles south of Mexico City. For three weeks they kept on the move, eluding police and police informers and finally returning to Mexico City by a circuitous route. There they holed up in a friend's apartment.

There is evidence that by this time Sara regretted any connection she had with the gang, and may have made an effort to contact the police. In any case, on 5 May 1989 the police became aware of a woman answering Sara's description, buying a large amount of groceries from various food stores. Gradually the police's net tightened.

On the morning of 6 May a lookout spotted a known police officer in plain clothes. Constanzo joined the lookout at the window and was able to pick out a number of officers moving into strategic positions. Suddenly Constanzo went berserk. 'They're here! Why run? Don't hide!' screamed the Godfather. He began to run around the flat, gathering up piles of coins and sheaves of US $20, $50 and $100 bills, flinging them through the window into the street.

Then, as passers-by ran forward to get at the money, he thrust an AK-47 out and began firing wildly, chipping chunks of masonry from the walls opposite and reducing a tamale cart to matchwood.

There followed an intense forty-five minute gunbattle, with Alvaro de Leon Valdez taking over Constanzo's gun while the Godfather himself continued to panic, burning wads of money on the gas stove and screaming, 'Let's all die!'

Finally Constanzo grabbed his homosexual lover, Martin Quintana, and hustled him into a cupboard, where the two men embraced before Constanzo ordered Valdez to kill them both.

After some persuasion, Valdez turned the AK-47 on to his chief, and sprayed the two men with bullets, killing them instantly. Valdez, Sara and the rest surrendered shortly afterwards.

In the early 1990s, the trials arising from the bizarre Constanzo affair are still proceeding. In August 1990 Alvaro de Leon Valdez was sentenced to thirty years for killing Constanzo and Quintana. Sara Maria Aldrete was acquitted on these charges but given six years for criminal association. Most of the other gang members remain in jail, awaiting final sentence.

The reaction of Helen Kilroy, Mark's mother, to the horrors of the Santa Elena ranch was almost superhumanly charitable. 'I think they must be possessed by the devil,' said the Catholic Irishwoman. 'That is the only explanation for what they did. I pray for all of them.'

COMMANDANTE AYALA TURNED WHITE MAGIC AGAINST BLACK TO DESTROY THE VOODOO TEMPLE

'LET'S ALL DIE!' SCREAMED THE HYSTERICAL CONSTANZO AS HE BURNED WADS OF MONEY ON A GAS STOVE

Below: *El Dubi is arrested in Mexico City following a shoot-out between police and Constanzo's cult members.*

PETER SUTCLIFFE
The Yorkshire Ripper

In the 1970s Yorkshire women were terrorized by a serial killer who, like the notorious Jack the Ripper, inflicted hideous mutilations on his victims. Was Peter Sutcliffe a paranoid schizophrenic, or just 'a wilfully evil bastard'?

Left: *Peter Sutcliffe at seven years old.*

Opposite: *Peter Sutcliffe, the Yorkshire Ripper, on his wedding day.*

Late on the afternoon of 22 May 1981, a dark-haired, bearded, scruffy little man rose to his feet in the dock beneath the dome of Number One Court at the Old Bailey to hear judgement passed upon him.

Found guilty of murdering thirteen women, and attempting to murder seven others, thirty-five-year-old Peter William Sutcliffe was sentenced to life imprisonment by Mr Justice Boreham with a recommendation that he should serve at least thirty years.

And yet, as the police knew to their unease, it was only by fluke that the 'Yorkshire Ripper' had been finally brought to book.

AN ORDINARY MURDER

The Ripper murders began in 1975 on a bitter morning of freezing fog in the rundown Chapeltown area of Leeds. A milkman making deliveries in Harrogate Road spotted a frosted bundle of what appeared to be rags on the white-rimed grass. He went and peered at it. It was a woman's body.

She lay on her back, her dyed blonde hair dark and spiky with dried blood. Her jacket and blouse had been torn open and her bra pulled up, revealing breasts and abdomen, and her trousers were round her knees, though her pants were still in position. Her torso had been stabbed and slashed fourteen times, after her death from two crushing hammer blows to the back of the skull.

The dead woman's name was Wilma McCann. She was twenty-eight years old, the mother of four young children, and separated from her husband.

Because Mrs McCann's purse was missing, West Yorkshire Metropolitan Police treated the case as murder in the pursuance of robbery. Despite the brutality of the attack there seemed no other motive.

DEATH OF A 'GOOD-TIME GIRL'

Just over two and a half months later, forty-two-year-old Emily Jackson set out with her husband from their home in the

THE MILKMAN THOUGHT THE PILE OF RAGS WAS AN ABANDONED GUY FAWKES FIGURE – WHEN HE LOOKED, HE SAW IT WAS A WOMAN'S BODY

Below: *Peter and Sonia Sutcliffe with friends on holiday.*

respectable village of Churwell, three miles south-west of Leeds, for a drink at the Gaiety pub on the Roundhay Road, Chapeltown.

In the 1970s Chapeltown was a red light area with a long pedigree. But not all the girls were local, nor were they all 'professionals'. Emily Jackson was one of many women who came to Chapeltown once or twice a week to sell herself on a casual basis. The police categorized these amateur prostitutes – and Wilma McCann had been an occasional member of their ranks – as 'good-time girls'.

On the early evening of 20 January 1976 Emily and her husband arrived at the Gaiety and had a drink together before Emily went off 'trolling' for custom. An hour after her arrival, her husband saw her get into a Land Rover in the pub car park. He drank in the pub until closing time, and then went home.

Early next morning a worker going onshift came across a bundle with a coat over it. He lifted the coat and found Emily Jackson, lying on her back.

Like Wilma McCann she had been killed from behind by two blows from a heavy hammer. Her breasts were exposed and her trousers pulled down, though again her pants were in place. On her right thigh was stamped the impression of a heavily ribbed wellington boot.

The similarity of her wounds with those of Wilma McCann was so close that police knew they were dealing with a

Above: *The Royal Standard pub where Peter and Sonia Sutcliffe first met.*

Below: *Peter Sutcliffe prepares to carry his new bride over the threshold.*

double murderer. The only solid clue they had so far was that the perpetrator took size seven in shoes.

SERIAL KILLER ON THE LOOSE

Over a year went by. Though the murder files remained open at Millgarth, the Leeds headquarters of the West Yorkshire police, no progress was made. Then, on 5 February 1977, the killer struck again.

His third victim was twenty-eight-year-old Irene Richardson, another 'good-time girl'. She was discovered by a jogger on Soldiers' Field, not far from Chapeltown. She was lying on her face and had died from three hammer blows to the back of her skull. Her killer had stripped her from the waist downwards. Her neck and chest had been subjected to a frenzied knife attack.

The pattern of wounds now left no doubt that the police were dealing with a serial killer.

As details of the killings spread through the street-girl population, many prostitutes, amateur and professional, began either to stay off the streets or to move to other cities.

Not so, however, with the Manningham

VICTIM 1
... McCann, 28,
...ds prostitute

VICTIM 2
Joan Harrison, 26,
Preston prostitute

VICTIM 3
Emily Jackson, 42,
Leeds prostitute

VICTIM 4
Irene Richardson, 28,
Leeds prostitute

...IM 5
...Atkinson, 33,
...ford prostitute

VICTIM 6
Jayne McDonald, 16,
Leeds shopgirl

VICTIM 7
Jean Royle,
prostitute, 21

VICTIM 8
Helen Rytka
prostitute, 18

...M 9
...e Pearson, 21,
...ord prostitute

VICTIM 10
Vera Millward,
prostitute, 40

VICTIM 11
Josie Whitaker, 19,
Halifax clerk

VICTIM 12
Barbara Leach, 20,
Bradford student

Jacqui, the last victim

Lane–Lumb Lane–Oak Lane triangle which served as the red light district of Bradford, some ten miles away. By the 1970s the district had been largely colonized by Asian immigrants who were making valiant efforts to modernize the semi-derelict properties.

But prostitutes did a steady trade there, often catering to the Asian businessmen whose religion and customs forbade them to sleep with their own women before

Above: *Ten of Sutcliffe's thirteen victims were prostitutes from Leeds or Bradford.*

ONCE AGAIN, THE KILLER HAD LEFT HIS 'SIGNATURE' - THE IMPRINT OF A SIZE SEVEN WELLINGTON BOOT

marriage. One such girl was thirty-two-year-old Patricia Atkinson.

On Saturday, 23 April, 'Tina' Atkinson set out for her local, the Carlisle. She enjoyed the noisy, friendly boozing spree, and lurched rather drunkenly back to her flat alone when the pub closed.

The following evening friends called for her, but got no answer to their ring on the doorbell. Since the door was ajar, they went in. Tina lay on her bed, the back of her head crushed by four hammer blows. She was naked. Seven knife wounds had lacerated her stomach, and her left-hand side had been slashed open.

Any doubts about the killer's identity were dispelled by a clue found imprinted on the bottom bedsheet. It was the mark of a size seven wellington boot, identical with the imprint found on Emily Jackson's thigh.

This serial killer seemed to have a particular antipathy towards prostitutes. The police began touring Chapeltown and Lumb Lane, questioning street girls about any regulars who might have acted suspiciously. Then, on Sunday, 26 June 1977, came an even nastier shock.

THE RIPPER SPREADS HIS NET

At 9.45a.m., a sixteen-year-old girl named Jayne MacDonald was found slumped and dead in Reginald Terrace, a street on the fringes of Chapeltown. Her long blonde hair was stained and tangled with blood from at least three hammer blows. She had been stabbed once in the back and several times through the chest. But Jayne MacDonald was no prostitute or good-time girl.

It now seemed certain that the Yorkshire Ripper regarded any woman out alone at night as fair game. A fortnight later this was emphasized when a Bradford housewife, Maureen Long, was struck down near her home but miraculously survived.

In the face of increasing public outcry the police stepped up their enquiries. Three hundred and four officers were assigned to the case. And to head them, veteran detective George Oldfield, Assistant Chief Constable (Crime), came out from behind his desk at administrative headquarters in Wakefield.

THE FIRST CLUE

The next time the Ripper struck he changed his location and killing pattern, but left a clue which was to bring him face to face with his hunters. Unfortunately for them, he slipped the net.

On 1 October 1977, a Saturday night, Jean Bernadette Jordan, a frail but experienced prostitute, was picked up near her home in Moss Side, Manchester and driven by her murderer to the Southern Cemetery two miles away. She demanded £5 in advance and was paid with a crisp new note, which she hid in a 'secret' pocket of her purse.

As she climbed from the Ripper's car on to allotment land adjoining the large cemetery, Mrs Jordan was knocked to the ground with a hammer blow and beaten eleven times more. Then she was pulled into a clump of bushes. But the killer was disturbed by the arrival of another car and made off.

The £5 note had been given to the Ripper in his wage packet two days before the attack. He realized that it might be a valuable clue, and eight days later returned to the Southern Cemetery area. After searching in vain for his victim's handbag, the Ripper attacked the decaying body with a ragged shard of broken glass.

Two days after the second attack, Mrs Jordan's remains were discovered, along with the missing handbag which had fallen among the bushes. The £5 note, serial number AW51 121565, had been used in the wage packets of the road haulage firm T. and W.H. Clark. And one of Clark's drivers was Peter Sutcliffe, who had worked there since October 1976.

LIVING VICTIMS

A month after he killed Jean Jordan, detectives visited Sutcliffe at his spacious detached home at 6 Garden Lane, Heaton, in one of the greener areas of Bradford.

Sutcliffe told them that he had lived there for three years since marrying his wife Sonia in 1974. He seemed a steady, quiet man, and the officers left, satisfied.

But had they had time and reason to do so, they would have discovered from old

Above: *Police examine the scene where Emily Jackson, the Ripper's third victim, was murdered.*

IT WAS WOUNDED MALE PRIDE THAT HAD LED SUTCLIFFE TO CARRY OUT HIS FIRST 'REVENGE' ATTACK ON A PROSTITUTE

Below: *Assistant Chief Constable George Oldfield and Superintendent Richard Holland at a 'Ripper' press conference.*

Bradford City Police files that Peter Sutcliffe had attacked his first victim in August 1969, and had been questioned by the police as a result. This first attack was not quite motiveless. Earlier that summer he had suspected his girlfriend Sonia of seeing another man.

To 'get even', he had approached a Bradford prostitute, but had been unable to maintain an erection. The woman had laughed at him, taken his £10, and got her pimp to chase him away.

In August he had seen her in the St Paul's red light district, crept after her, and hit her violently on the back of the head with a stone in a sock. The woman had noted the number of his van, and

Sutcliffe had been traced. But because he had no record, he had been let off with a caution.

Since then he had left five women damaged but alive. The first was Anna Rogulskyj, beaten with a hammer on 5 July 1975 in Keighley. The next victim was Olive Smelt, who was beaten down and slashed with a knife near her Halifax home on 15 August of the same year. On 9 May 1976 he had struck down Marcella Claxton, a West Indian prostitute from Chapeltown, and a fortnight after killing Jayne MacDonald he had attacked a woman named Maureen Long in Bradford. Later that year, on 14 December, he struck at Marilyn Moore in Leeds.

Each of these living victims had tried to describe their attacker. Mrs Smelt had been on the right track when she described him as thirtyish, about 5 ft 10 ins tall, and bearded. Marcella Claxton had described him accurately as having a black, crinkly beard, but because she was educationally subnormal her statement was treated less seriously.

DESPERATION

On the evening of 21 January 1978, a twenty-two-year-old 'career' prostitute named Yvonne Pearson went into Bradford to the Flying Dutchman pub in Lumb Lane.

At 9.30p.m. she left the pub and was

Below: Police search the alley where the body of Barbara Leach was discovered. A 20-year-old student, she was the Ripper's penultimate victim.

Bottom: Police search for clues in their hunt for the Yorkshire Ripper.

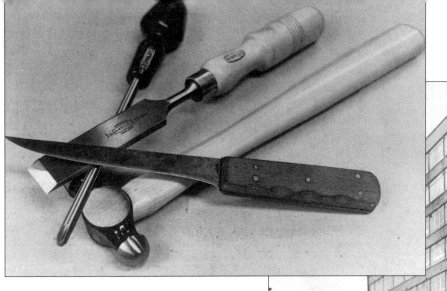

seen climbing into a car driven by a man described as having a dark beard and black, piercing eyes. It was Sutcliffe, who took her to waste ground in Arthington Street, killed her with a club hammer and jumped on her chest until her ribs cracked. He then piled an old abandoned horsehair sofa on top of her. About a month later, when the body remained undiscovered, Sutcliffe was to return and place a current copy of the *Daily Mirror* under one of her mouldering arms. But between the killing and the newspaper incident he had paid a visit to Huddersfield.

Helen and Rita Rytka were pretty eighteen-year-old twins, the product of an Italian mother and a Jamaican father. They had gained places at West Yorkshire art schools and had done well. Economic pressures, however, had forced them into a squalid Huddersfield bedsitter, and a life of prostitution.

Because of the Ripper publicity, Helen and Rita had worked out 'safety measures' including the taking of car numbers and the timing of 'tricks'. But on the snowy night of Tuesday, 31 January 1978, the safety net broke down.

While Rita was off with a client, Sutcliffe picked up Helen. They went into a timber yard under railway arches near the centre of the town and, uncharacteristically, Sutcliffe managed to have intercourse with her before killing her in his usual fashion.

Immediately after Helen Rytka's murder, the police were optimistic. Her abduction had taken place in the early evening on a busy street. But despite tracing a hundred passers by, and with all but three cars and one man eliminated, there was no real result.

Above left: *Peter Sutcliffe's murder weapons could have been bought at any local hardware store.*

Above: *The bus stop at Leeds' Arndale Shopping Centre where Jacqueline Hill was accosted and murdered by the Yorkshire Ripper.*

The police were convinced that the Ripper lived in the locality of Leeds or Bradford, but they little realized that, by the end of 1978, they had interviewed him no fewer than four times. Apart from two visits concerning the £5 note clue, they had called at Garden Lane because routine checks had turned up Sutcliffe's car registration in red light areas. They also called to check on tyre tracks to compare them with some found near the scene of Irene Richardson's murder.

But they did not check two vital clues they knew about the Ripper against Sutcliffe. The Ripper was a B secretor – a rare blood type. And he took size seven boots – very small for a man.

On the night of 16 May 1978, two months after Yvonne Pearson's body was found, Sutcliffe killed Vera Millward, a forty-one-year-old prostitute. Then, for eleven months, he lay quiet.

Then, as women were beginning to venture abroad again tragedy befell an ordinary Halifax family. Nineteen-year-old Josephine Whittaker, a clerk in the Halifax Building Society headquarters, was hurrying home across Savile Park playing fields when she was attacked and killed with sickeningly familiar ferocity. She was the second non-prostitute to die.

TAUNTS AND HOAXES

Between Josephine Whittaker's death in May 1979 and September of the same year there was another lull. This time it was filled by a brutal hoax which almost certainly cost three women their lives.

Since March 1978 George Oldfield had received two letters purporting to come from the Ripper. Shortly before the Whittaker murder a third letter came, mentioning Vera Millward's death. All three letters were postmarked from Sunderland in the north-east. On the third traces of engineering oil, similar to traces found on Josephine Whittaker's body, were discovered. To the beleaguered detectives, this seemed to confirm that the letters were written by the Ripper.

When, on 18 June 1979, a tape recording addressed in the same handwriting as the letters was received, West Yorkshire police were convinced

*Above: **Peter and Sonia Sutcliffe's house in Garden Lane, Heston, Bradford.***

that they had all but got their man. The tape, a taunting message to Oldfield personally, was in a broad Geordie accent, narrowed down by experts to one small town in Sunderland called Castletown. The West Yorkshire police became convinced that anyone without a Geordie accent could be eliminated from their enquiry. This, of course, put Sutcliffe temporarily in the clear.

In July he was visited by Detective Constable Laptew, who had noticed that Sutcliffe's car had been spotted in the Lumb Lane area on thirty-six separate occasions. Laptew was deeply suspicious of Sutcliffe, but because of the Sunderland connection he went unheeded by his superiors.

On the late evening of 1 September 1979 Sutcliffe ambushed a social sciences student named Barbara Leach in the residential area of Little Horton in

OBSESSED WITH THE 'SUNDERLAND CONNECTION', THE POLICE DISREGARDED ONE OFFICER'S DEEP SUSPICIONS OF SUTCLIFFE

Left: *Police dig up Peter Sutcliffe's garden shortly after his arrest on suspicion of being the Yorkshire Ripper.*

Bradford as she left a friendly pub called the Mannville Arms.

On 18 August 1980 Sutcliffe killed for the twelfth time, his victim was forty-seven-year-old civil servant Margaret Walls. Because she had been bludgeoned and strangled, but not mutilated further, the Ripper Squad were reluctant to add her to their list of victims. But there was no question of the authenticity of his thirteenth and final slaying.

Twenty-year-old Jacqueline Hill, a language student at Leeds University, was walking home to Lupton Flats, a hall of residence in respectable Otley Road, Leeds, when she was spotted by Peter Sutcliffe. He dragged her on to waste land and savaged her with a hammer, a knife and a screwdriver.

The casual pointlessness of Jacqueline Hill's brutal death caused a backlash of frustration among the public and police.

As a sop to police feeling, the Home Office set up a 'super squad' of four outside detectives and a forensic scientist, Mr Stuart Kind. The idea was that this team should review the evidence, and in fact they made some progress. For instance, they deduced that the 'Geordie' letters and tape must be a hoax, and computer calculations pinpointed the 'centre of gravity' of the Ripper's operations as Bradford. A final sweep, using blood group, shoe size, tyre tracks and the £5 note 'wage packet' clue might well, inexorably, have nailed the wretched Sutcliffe.

As it was, he was caught by chance. On 2 January 1981, Sergeant Robert Ring and Police Constable Robert Hydes of South Yorkshire Police were cruising along Melbourne Avenue, Sheffield – a haunt of prostitutes – when they saw a girl getting into a Rover V8 3500.

Below: *There was tight security as a crowd assembled to watch the arrival of Peter Sutcliffe at Dewsbury Magistrates' Court.*

Left: *Police help Sonia Sutcliffe as she enters Dewsbury Court for her husband's hearing.*

SUTCLIFFE CLAIMED THAT A VOICE IN A GRAVEYARD HAD ORDERED HIM TO GO OUT AND KILL PROSTITUTES

Below: *Peter Sutcliffe after being attacked in prison.*

The driver, a short, bearded man, gave his name as Peter Williams and asked if he could relieve himself before answering further questions. Bob Ring nodded, and the man disappeared into bushes by the side of the road.

After being interviewed at Sheffield, 'Williams' was driven to Dewsbury in West Yorkshire for further questioning, because it had been discovered that his number plates were false and had been stolen from that town. Later that day, when Sergeant Ring heard that the driver was still being held at Dewsbury, the implication struck him.

He dashed back to Melbourne Avenue and searched the bushes. There he found a ball-peen hammer and a knife, which eventually were to be matched to the Ripper's crimes.

'Well, it's me,' he told the Dewsbury police. 'I'm glad it's all over. I would have killed that girl if I hadn't been caught.'

What made him do it? Sutcliffe himself told how he had been cheated by the prostitute back in 1969, later claiming that, when he was a gravedigger in the early seventies at Bingley cemetery, a voice emanating from a gravestone had told him to go out and kill prostitutes.

Some experts argued that he was a paranoid schizophrenic who had little control over the delusions and impulses that haunted him, while one of the Home Office pathologists who worked on the case echoed the thoughts of the general public: 'He was quite simply a wilfully evil bastard.'

While awaiting trial in Armley gaol, Leeds, Sutcliffe was overheard by a warder planning with his wife Sonia that he would fake 'madness' and 'be out in ten years'. As it was, his plot failed. He was sent to Parkhurst maximum security prison on the Isle of Wight.

Peter Sutcliffe's mental condition did begin to deteriorate, and in March 1984 he was moved to Ward One of Somerset House, Broadmoor Institution for the Criminally Insane, where, in the early 1990s, he remains.

JOHN CHRISTIE
10 Rillington Place

Ridiculed for sexual inadequacy, the warped John Christie developed into a necrophiliac murderer, walling up his victims in a squalid London flat. In the process, he was a part in one of Britain's worst-ever miscarriages of justice

In March 1953 a Jamaican couple, Mr Beresford Brown and his wife, received good news from their landlord. For some years the Browns had rented cramped rooms on the third floor of 10 Rillington Place, a decaying property in the Ladbroke Grove area of North Kensington in west London.

Would the Browns like to move to the ground floor? Mr and Mrs Brown were delighted. The ground-floor flat had a front room, a bedroom and a kitchen as well as a wash house, and the single lavatory shared by all the tenants was on the ground floor too. There was even a small garden out at the back.

The only slight misgiving was felt by Mrs Brown. She had often seen John Christie sprinkling strong disinfectant around the flat and along the corridor which connected the front door with the back yard.

There was also the reputation of 10 Rillington Place. Five years previously the second-floor tenant, Timothy Evans, had been charged with killing his wife and infant daughter in the house. He had been hanged for the murders in 1949.

For some days Beresford Brown worked hard, removing piles of old clothes, decaying furniture and general rubbish from the kitchen and heaping it in the back garden. Finally, on 24 March, the room was stripped to its bare walls. Brown began tapping the plaster of the rear wall, but it sounded strangely hollow. He stripped off a piece of mouldering wallpaper and found that it covered a cupboard door. Behind the wooden door was an alcove, and Brown's torch shone on the bare back and buttocks of a woman. She was hunched forward, and wore only a bra, a white cotton coat, stockings and suspender belt. The unnatural colour of her flesh, and the stench, clearly indicated that she had occupied her impromptu tomb for some time.

Right: *The body of Mrs Ethel Christie was found under the floorboards in the living-room of 10 Rillington Place.*

The police came around quickly to continue the search. Behind the first body they found a second corpse, wrapped in a blanket, and beyond that a third, also wrapped in a blanket which had been tied with electric flex.

The search went on into the night, and in the early hours of the following day a fourth body was found wrapped in a blanket and stuffed beneath the floorboards of the front room. She was identified as Mrs Ethel Christie, and like the rest of the corpses she had been strangled.

As forensic experts were called in, the police called a press conference. They had uncovered, they said, the 'most brutal mass killing known in London', and they were looking for a 'vital witness'. His name was John Reginald Halliday Christie, aged fifty-four. He and his wife had lived at 10 Rillington Place since 1938.

Digging in the garden revealed two more female skeletons. The skull of one was missing, and the thigh bone of another had been used to prop up a fence. Meanwhile, undetected, John Christie wandered around London.

On 31 March, Police Constable V100 Thomas Ledger made himself the most famous copper in the land. On his beat near Putney Bridge he saw a short, middle-aged man in a trilby hat leaning over the embankment railings by the Star and Garter Hotel.

'Can you tell me who you are?' asked PC Ledger.

'John Waddington, 35 Westbourne Grove,' said the man.

PC Ledger asked him to remove his hat. The bald head thus revealed confirmed the officer's suspicions, and John Christie was under arrest.

YORKSHIRE ORIGINS

Christie was born on 8 April 1898 in Halifax, West Yorkshire, where his father Ernest was a designer for one of the town's leading firms, Crossley Carpets. Ernest Christie was an upright, no-nonsense Victorian figure, a founder of the Halifax Conservative Party.

Not surprisingly John, one of seven children, lived in mortal fear of his father.

> THEY HAD UNCOVERED, SAID THE POLICE, 'THE MOST BRUTAL MASS KILLING KNOWN IN LONDON'

On the other hand his mother enveloped her children with affection. Four of Christie's siblings were sisters, three of them older than himself. They, too, tended to suffocate young John with perhaps misguided kindness.

John Christie went to Sunday School, sang in the choir and became a Boy Scout, rising to the rank of assistant

scoutmaster. At secondary school he was good at arithmetic and algebra and meticulously neat in his work. He was also good with his hands, making toys and repairing watches.

After he left school at fourteen, Christie's early facade of respectability seemed to crumble. One day, working in the Gem Cinema in Halifax, he was picked up by an older, sexually experienced girl and taken to an alley known locally as the Monkey Run. Christie failed to get an erection, and the girl spread the word; overnight he was known as 'Reggie-No-Dick' or 'Can't-Do-It-Reggie'.

There is no doubt that this incident had a direct bearing on the direction of his feelings towards women. 'Women who give you the come-on look,' he told a psychiatrist while in Brixton, 'wouldn't look nearly so saucy if they were helpless and dead.'

FROM PETTY CRIME TO MURDER

Sex was only the first of a line of disasters. At seventeen he got a job as civilian clerk with the West Riding Constabulary, but was sacked for fiddling the petty cash.

For the next few months he drifted from job to job, mainly as a clerk, until in 1916, during the First World War, he was called up and sent to France. In June 1918 he was gassed and invalided out of the army.

Marriage in May 1920 to a plump, amiable girl from Leeds named Edith Waddington seemed to do little to curb Christie's petty criminal ways. A job as postman ended when he was caught stealing money from packets and imprisoned for nine months. Two years later he was bound over for violence and in 1924, having drifted south, he was jailed for a further nine months for larceny at Uxbridge Petty Sessions.

For the next ten years, Christie's life continued its aimless course. Ethel left him, and for a while he lived with a prostitute until he beat her up so badly that he was sentenced to six months' hard labour. Magistrates called it a 'murderous attack'. It was not to be the last.

The placid Ethel returned to him, however, and seems to have kept him at least outwardly respectable as they settled at Rillington Place.

Despite his criminal record, Christie spent the Second World War in the Emergency Reserve as a special constable at Harrow Road police station in west London.

It was in the early summer of 1943, looking for a man wanted for theft, among the low-life cafés and pubs of Notting Hill, that John Christie met his first victim. Her name was Ruth Fuerst and she was a tall, dark-haired Austrian, a refugee from Hitler.

Curiously enough, Christie had a knack for drawing out confidences from women. He sat with Ruth in a café and listened sympathetically to her problems, even lending her ten shillings.

They continued to meet for several

Above: *Rillington Place in Notting Hill, an address made famous by Ludovic Kennedy in his book of the same name.*

IN SPITE OF HIS RECORD OF THEFT AND VIOLENCE, DURING THE SECOND WORLD WAR CHRISTIE WAS TAKEN ON AS A SPECIAL CONSTABLE

months. And then one hot afternoon in August, when Ethel was safely away visiting relatives in Sheffield, he invited Ruth back to 10 Rillington Place.

'I was rather backward and shy about the act of lovemaking on this occasion,' he was to admit, 'but she was encouraging.' The couple went to the Christies' matrimonial bed, and there, during intercourse, he strangled her with a piece of rope.

As Christie struggled to clean up the evidence of his act, the doorbell rang. It was a telegraph boy with a message announcing that Ethel was coming back.

Christie hastily prised up the floorboards of the front room and hid the body and clothes there.

Ethel returned with her brother Henry. That night Henry slept in the front room, inches above the stiffening corpse of Ruth Fuerst, while Ethel and Christie lay together in the murder bed.

The next day Christie removed the body to the wash house, and spent the afternoon digging a grave in the garden. Neighbours, he recalled, waved to him at his labours. Under cover of darkness he buried Ruth.

THE SECOND VICTIM

At the end of 1943 Christie, perhaps uneasy about what he had done, applied for a release from the police force. In January 1944 he took a civilian job at the Ultra Radio Works in Park Royal, Acton.

There he befriended a girl from the despatch department named Muriel Amelia Eady.

Muriel was thirty-one and a highly respectable spinster who lived with her aunt in Putney. She often sat next to Christie in the canteen, and soon, with his knack of inspiring confidences, he learned that her father was in the Royal Navy and she had a boyfriend.

The boyfriend gave Christie cover – an excuse to invite them both to tea at Rillington Place to meet Ethel. He had already decided that plump and homely Muriel was to go the way of Ruth Fuerst.

First, however, he had to find a method of getting her alone and subduing her without violence. In the autumn, he saw a solution to both problems. Muriel suffered from chronic catarrh, and Christie was able to convince her, with his knowledge of first aid, that he had a remedy.

In October Ethel went off to Sheffield again, and Christie seized his opportunity. He had rigged up a screw-top jar with two rubber tubes leading from it, one to a face mask and the other, secretly, to a gas tap.

Christie invited Muriel round, and, over a cup of tea, persuaded her that the apparatus would help her catarrh.

IN THEIR CRAMPED QUARTERS MARRIED BLISS COULD NOT LAST, AND SOON TIMOTHY AND BERYL WERE HAVING VIOLENT QUARRELS

*Below: **Chief Inspector Griffin and Inspector Kelly leaving 10 Rillington Place after the discovery of the bodies.***

Obediently, Muriel inhaled – the jar was filled with Friar's Balsam, to mask the smell of gas – and when she lapsed into unconsciousness, he carried her into the bedroom and strangled her during the sexual act. Afterwards he buried her alongside Ruth Fuerst.

At Easter 1948 a young couple named Timothy and Beryl Evans rented the top flat at Rillington Place. Beryl was pregnant, and the pair were eager to settle anywhere.

In October 1948 Beryl gave birth to a baby daughter. She was named Geraldine, and both Timothy and Beryl adored her.

For a while the trio were happy at Rillington Place. Unfortunately, it was not to last. Like other married couples in cramped quarters the Evanses had their quarrels, sometimes violent.

On one occasion, Beryl invited a girlfriend to stay. The two women slept in the bed, which meant that Timothy had to rough it on the floor. The following day a flurry of blows were struck. To make matters worse, Beryl began to neglect the housework, and the tiny flat became untidy and dirty.

THE ABORTION THAT WENT WRONG

In the summer of 1949 Beryl, to her horror, became pregnant again. She wanted an abortion, but Timothy and his mother, both Catholics, were against it. In desperation Beryl told Christie. He persuaded her that, with his 'medical training', he could do the operation.

Evans was furious when Beryl told him, but was somewhat mollified when Christie showed him one of his 'medical books' – an old St John Ambulance Brigade manual. Timothy, who was almost totally illiterate, was impressed by the pictures and reluctantly agreed to Christie 'taking care of' Beryl.

On either 6 or 7 November 1949, Evans came home to find Christie waiting for him. The operation had gone wrong, and Beryl was dead.

Without giving the bewildered Timothy time for grief or remonstrance, Christie told him that if he went to the police he, Christie, would be charged with manslaughter or possibly murder, as

Above: *The house where Christie lived as a child.*

Left: *Christie in his uniform. He served as a special constable during the Second World War.*

purchase – for £40, and destroyed the bloodstained sheets on which his wife had died. He then told Christie he was going to Bristol, but instead went to South Wales, where he stayed with his aunt and uncle.

If Evans naively expected to leave his troubles behind and find peace in his native valleys, he was mistaken. He told his family that Beryl had walked out.

Finally, on 30 November 1949, he decided to go to Merthyr Vale police station. There, his habitual lying got him into an inextricable mess.

First, he told a detective constable that he had disposed of his wife. Then he said that it had been an accident, that, to procure a miscarriage, he had bought a bottle of chemicals from a man in a transport café in East Anglia.

He had told his wife not to drink the contents of the bottle, but she had done so. When he got home he had found her dead and had thrust her body, under cover of darkness, down a drainage manhole in the road outside the house.

The Merthyr Vale police contacted the Metropolitan Police, and men from Notting Hill station went to Rillington Place. The drain was empty. Faced with this weighty contradiction, Evans made another statement, implicating Christie in the abortion.

FRAMED FOR MURDER

When interviewed, Christie skilfully used his knowledge of the police mind to slip Evans into trouble while extricating himself. He told of the couple's rows and the exchange of blows. He said that Beryl had accused her husband of trying to throttle her.

A search of the premises revealed Beryl's body in the wash house, wrapped in a green tablecloth behind a stack of wood. The body of baby Geraldine was found behind the door, with a tie tightly knotted around her neck.

The Home Office pathologist, Dr Donald Teare, reported that both victims had died of strangulation. Beryl's right eye and upper lip were badly swollen and there were signs of bruising in her vagina, though Dr Teare omitted to take a vaginal swab. Had he done so, things

abortion was illegal. Slyly he got Evans to help him move Beryl's body to the second floor flat whose occupant was in hospital. Now Timothy Evans was an accessory to murder.

Christie promised that he and Ethel would find someone to look after Evans' baby daughter. He also promised to help Evans by putting Beryl's body down a drainage shaft in the street outside.

During the next few days, Evans sold the furniture – which was still on hire

> CHRISTIE GOT EVANS TO HELP HIM MOVE BERYL'S BODY TO AN EMPTY FLAT – NOW EVANS WAS AN ACCESSORY TO MURDER

might have turned out differently, in view of John Christie's sexual habits.

As it was, the police now viewed the case as a simple 'domestic' which had turned into murder. Evans was brought back to Notting Hill and made two lengthy statements in the course of the afternoon of Friday, 2 December.

In his first, he claimed to have strangled Beryl and Geraldine while the Christies were in bed. In the second, he added that Beryl had been getting deeper and deeper into debt. The Crown decided to proceed only on the killing of Geraldine, a crime for which Evans could expect little sympathy.

Timothy Evans's trial for murder began at Number One Court at the Old Bailey on 11 January 1950, before Mr Justice Lewis.

In the witness box, Christie won the judge's sympathy when he told him that First World War gas had left him with difficulty in speaking. He also impressed him with an account of his wartime service as a special constable.

In the end the jury took just forty minutes to find Evans guilty of murder, and he was sentenced to death.

Thereafter – to his solicitors, counsel, family, priests and prison officers – Evans maintained the story that Christie had killed both Beryl and Geraldine. Already there was some public disquiet, and a petition with about 1800 signatures was presented to the Home Secretary.

But no reprieve was forthcoming. On 9 March, 1950, a bewildered Timothy Evans walked to the gallows. To the end he repeated his protest: 'I didn't do it. Christie done it.'

CHRISTIE ON THE LOOSE AGAIN

Almost two years after Timothy Evans's execution, the urge to kill came upon John Christie once again. This time, the victim was his wife Ethel.

On 14 December 1952, Christie was to claim that he was awakened by his prematurely elderly and arthritic wife having convulsions. To put her out of her misery 'in the kindest way', he strangled her. 'For two days I left my wife's body in bed. Then I pulled up the floorboards of the front room and buried her.'

Afterwards, said Christie, he was sorry. 'From the first day I missed her. The quiet love she and I bore each other happens only once in a lifetime.'

During the few weeks after Ethel's killing, he sold most of his furniture and lived with a few bare essentials, accompanied only by his cat and mongrel bitch Judy, to which he was devoted. At Christmas he sent Ethel's sister and her husband in Sheffield a Christmas card signed 'From Ethel and Reg'.

That winter he prowled the streets and cafés of Notting Hill as he had done in

Above: *Timothy Evans, Christie's tragic dupe, gave himself up to police in Merthyr Vale and was shipped back to London to face murder charges.*

wartime. By March 1953, he had lured three more women to their deaths in 10 Rillington Place.

The first was a twenty-six-year-old Southampton-born prostitute named Kathleen Maloney. After giving her the 'gas' treatment, as she lolled semi-conscious in a deckchair, Christie strangled her during sex. Then, after wrapping her in a blanket, he thrust her into the kitchen alcove and papered over the door.

A few days later, Christie struck again. This time his victim was a twenty-five-year-old Belfast street-walker named Rita Nelson whom he met in a café. She was gassed, strangled and ravished, then pushed in behind Kathleen Maloney.

Towards the end of February Christie came across Hectorina MacLennan, fated to be his last victim. Hectorina, a twenty-six-year-old originally from Scotland, was living with her lorry driver boyfriend Alexander Baker, but the couple had been locked out of their flat. Christie invited Hectorina back to Rillington Place, but was disconcerted when she turned up with Baker in tow.

The three of them spent an extremely uncomfortable three days together in the first week in March. Although the couple were lovers, Christie would not allow them to use his mattress. While one slept, the other sat up with him in the kitchen – for despite his necrophiliac preferences, a streak of puritanism from his long-gone Sunday school days in Halifax remained.

On 6 March Christie apparently accompanied the couple to the labour exchange. When Baker went in to sign for his dole money, Christie whisked Hectorina back to Rillington Place with him. When it was over, Christie shoved the still-warm MacLennan into the cupboard alcove, clipping her bra strap round Maloney's knees to hold her body upright. Then he sealed up the door again.

CONFESSION TIME

And then, it seemed, Christie had had enough of the dilapidated house and its mouldering ghosts. He fled, he was arrested and he began to confess – in letters to friends, to newspapers and to the police.

But even now the wily streak in his character was not subdued, for his very confessions were preparations towards the defence which he was convinced would see him clear of the gallows. He intended to prove that he was insane.

Christie's trial began on 22 June 1953 in the same Old Bailey court in which Evans had stood trial three years before.

Derek Curtis-Bennett QC, his distinguished defence counsel, was out to prove insanity on Christie's behalf. To this end Christie had admitted to all the women's murders, even that of Beryl Evans – 'The more the merrier,' he remarked. But, like Evans, he could expect scant sympathy for killing a child, so Curtis-Bennett tried to keep Geraldine's death out of the way.

The legal establishment were not, in any case, eager to awaken the spectre of a man who had perhaps been wrongly convicted and executed.

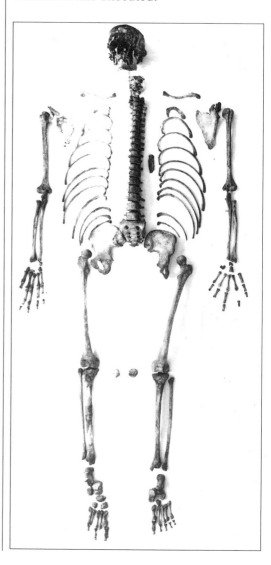

Right: *The skeleton of Ruth Fuerst found in the garden at 10 Rillington Place.*

efforts of his defence team, his trial lasted only four days, and at the end of it, on 25 June 1953, Christie was sentenced to death.

CAMPAIGN FOR TIMOTHY EVANS

Almost immediately, a clamour went up for a review of the Evans case. Under pressure from the Labour opposition the Home Secretary, Sir David Maxwell Fyfe, appointed the Recorder of Portsmouth, John Scott-Henderson, to study 'whether there is any ground for thinking there may have been a miscarriage of justice'. It was a monumental task which had to be completed in under twenty days, before sentence on Christie was carried out.

Surprisingly, when the hastily assembled report appeared it claimed that Evans had indeed carried out the murder of his daughter, as charged. But it added that he had also killed his wife. In other words, according to Scott-Henderson, Christie had told the truth at Evans's trial but lied at his own.

Although some criminologists have continued to have misgivings as to Evans's total innocence, a sustained campaign throughout the 1950s and into the 1960s by such journalists as Harold Evans and Ludovic Kennedy eventually bore fruit.

In 1966, a year after he had successfully called for the temporary abolition of capital punishment, Labour Home Secretary Roy Jenkins granted Timothy Evans a posthumous free pardon. On 18 October of that year, his remains were reburied at St Patrick's Cemetery in Leytonstone in east London. Four years later, capital punishment was abolished entirely.

Rillington Place lingered on for another half dozen years under a new name, Ruston Close. Finally it was demolished, and a new street, Bartle Road, built on its site. There is no number 10 at Bartle Road. A garden marks the spot, between number 9 and number 11, where the most infamous house in British criminal history once stood.

On 18 May, Beryl Evans's body had been exhumed from Kensington Borough Cemetery in Gunnersbury for examination by a trio of the leading Home Office consultant pathologists. The body of Geraldine, which lay alongside that of her mother, had not been exhumed.

The bones in the garden had been reassembled, and the heat-shattered skull of Ruth Fuerst was pieced together like a jigsaw puzzle. In post-mortem examinations, the bodies of Maloney, Nelson and MacLennan had been found to contain samples of Christie's sperm. But whether intercourse had taken place before, after or during the murders was impossible to prove.

In court, when he was asked if he had killed the baby Geraldine, Christie replied 'No.' He was constantly evasive about the evidence he had given in the Evans trial. In any case, despite the best

Above: *The wash house where baby Geraldine's body was found.*

THE REVIEW OF THE TIMOTHY EVANS CASE HAD TO BE COMPLETED IN A STAGGERING TWENTY DAYS, BEFORE CHRISTIE WAS DUE TO BE EXECUTED

PETER KURTEN
Düsseldorf Monster

Vampirism, cannibalism, rape and torture were all part of the depraved Peter Kurten's repertoire. After forty years of violence, bestiality and blood-lust he became the first serial killer to be examined in depth by a criminal psychiatrist

'I have no remorse. As to whether recollection of my deeds makes me feel ashamed, I will tell you. Thinking back to all the details is not at all unpleasant. I rather enjoy it.'

Thus, in the summer of 1931, spoke a polite, quiet-voiced, neat little man of forty-eight named Peter Kurten, who in a career spanning over thirty years had turned his adopted city of Düsseldorf into the murder centre of Europe. Kurten's name entered the annals of criminology

Right: Passers-by read the news of another murder in Düsseldorf.

Opposite: Peter Kurten was to become the most infamous murderer in the city's history.

Below left: The flat in Düsseldorf where Kurten and his wife lived.

Below: Kurten was regarded by his neighbours as a pleasant and likeable man.

through the fact that, after his conviction, he became the first serial killer ever interviewed in depth by a psychiatrist.

Professor Karl Berg concluded, after listening to Kurten's lucid and rational confession, that, though sane under German law, Kurten was a 'narcissistic psychopath' whose sole reason for being was the gratification of his own desires. It was the horrific variety of those desires that appalled the pre-Hitler German people: vampirism, cannibalism, bestiality, rape, sadism and murder in many forms.

PRECOCIOUS SEXUALITY

Peter Kurten was born in Köln-Mulheim in 1883 into a family of thirteen children. His father was a violent drunk, who often forced his wife to have sexual intercourse in front of his children. When finally he attempted sex with one of his daughters, his wife had him arrested and he was imprisoned.

But there is little doubt that a strange seed had been sown in the mind of Peter by the activities of his father. And that seed was nurtured by the town dog-catcher, who moved in as lodger when his father went to jail.

Kurten was a precociously sexual child. When his father was taken away he tried to molest the sister who had been attacked, imitating what he had seen his father do. The dog-catcher taught him to masturbate dogs and torture them.

Kurten was also a murderer very early on. At the age of nine, on a school outing in Düsseldorf, to which city the family had moved, he managed to push a friend off a raft. The friend could not swim, and when another boy dived in Kurten held his head under. Both boys drowned, but the blame was not lodged with Kurten until he confessed all to Professor Berg nearly forty years later.

At thirteen, Kurten began to practise bestiality with sheep, pigs and goats. Three years later he ran away from home to Koblenz, where he moved in with a prostitute. After stealing money from her he was jailed, the first of several prison sentences which were to take up over twenty years of his life.

EVIL FANTASIES

While in jail – much of the time in solitary confinement for insubordination – he began to fantasize. Once out, he tried an experiment by strangling a girl in a wood while having sex with her. As no body was ever found, it is presumed that this first victim, at least, escaped with her life and recovered.

By 1900 Kurten, just seventeen, was back in jail serving four years for theft. When he was released in 1904 his dark fantasies bore fruit. He committed his first recorded sex murder, getting away with it almost by fluke.

A ten-year-old girl named Christine Klein lived with her father in the family tavern at Köln-Mulheim, on the Rhine. One summer morning the girl was found dead, throttled into unconsciousness, and then slashed across the throat with a sharp knife. She had not been raped, but had suffered some sexual molestation.

Twice after the Klein killing, Peter Kurten struck down strangers in the street with an axe. Both victims survived. Kurten said he derived sexual pleasure from watching their blood flow.

In 1921 he was released from prison for burglary, and at his sister's house in Altenburg met his future wife. Posing as a prisoner of war recently released by the Russians, he wooed her with a mixture of sexual flattery and threats of violence.

Frau Kurten remains a shadowy figure. It appeared that she had been a prostitute for a time, and had been imprisoned for four years for shooting dead a man who had jilted her after promising marriage.

Kurten treated her with a kind of rough

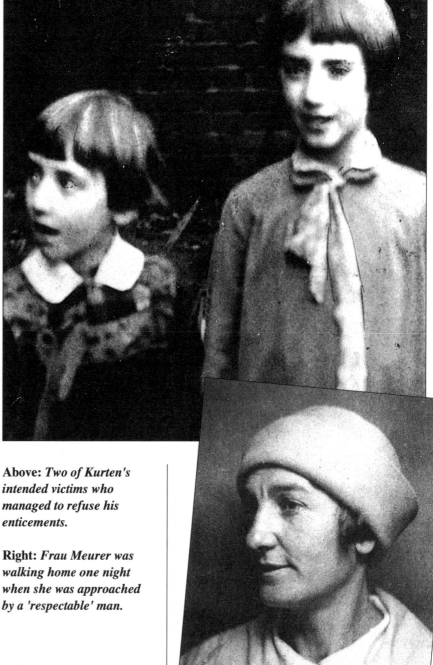

Above: *Two of Kurten's intended victims who managed to refuse his enticements.*

Right: *Frau Meurer was walking home one night when she was approached by a 'respectable' man.*

A MURDERER AT NINE, FOUR YEARS LATER KURTEN WAS INDULGING IN TORTURE AND BESTIALITY WITH FARMYARD ANIMALS

ARMED WITH AN AXE, KURTEN ATTACKED STRANGERS IN THE STREET - WATCHING THEIR BLOOD FLOW, HE SAID, GAVE HIM SEXUAL PLEASURE

---

affection, and although he was unfaithful always returned. For four years the couple lived in Altenburg, and Kurten made an effort to reform. He worked as a moulder, became a trade unionist, and was politically active in the troubled days of the ill-fated Weimar Republic.

From time to time, however, he still went on the prowl, seeking out women either to beat or to strangle into submission. Often, if he achieved orgasm before they passed out, he would apologize, saying; 'Ah well, that's the way love is.' Occasionally his wife intervened to save him from charges of assault.

NOCTURNAL ATROCITIES

Kurten realized, however, that his strange desires were growing again, and that Altenburg was too small a town for them to go undetected. In 1925 the Kurtens moved to Düsseldorf and settled in a top-floor flat at 71 Mettmannerstrasse. Almost at once, a series of sexual atrocities and murders made police aware that a maniac was roaming the streets.

They began on the night of 3 February 1929, when Kurten sprang from the shadows at a woman walking home and stabbed her twenty-four times with a pair of scissors. Miraculously, she survived. On 13 February, a forty-five-year-old mechanic named Rudolf Scheer was attacked on his way home from a beer cellar. He was stabbed repeatedly in the head and neck before being left to die in the road.

On the night of 9 March, Kurten had time to kill undisturbed. His victim was an eight-year-old girl named Rosa Ohliger, who was dragged behind a hedge and stabbed thirteen times.

Soon after this, Kurten had another lucky break. Two women were attacked by a man with a noose but escaped, badly bruised. They described their attacker as an 'idiot' with a hare-lip.

The police found a man named Stausberg who fitted the description. After confessing not only to the noose attacks but to the recent murders, he was confined to a mental home. For the next few months the attacks ceased and the police relaxed their vigilance.

But early in August 1929 they began again. Two women and a man were attacked as they walked home late at night. They survived.

Then, on the 24th, two children were found dead on an allotment in Düsseldorf. Like Christine Klein sixteen years before, they had been first throttled, then slashed across their throats.

That same afternoon, a serving maid named Gertrude Schulte was walking home when she was accosted by what she described as a 'pleasant-looking, ordinary man' of about forty. The man asked her outright to have sexual intercourse with her, walking by her side and almost pleading.

'I'd rather die!' said Gertrude. 'Well, die then!' said the man, and stabbed her several times before running off. She survived to give the police their first good description of the man they sought.

Kurten's next victim was not discovered until the late autumn. Another servant girl, twenty-year-old Maria Hahn, had been stabbed to death with twenty knife blows, and buried on the banks of the Rhine.

The following day Kurten returned to the site and dug up the body, intending, he said, to crucify it on a tree 'to shock passers-by'. But the body was too heavy, so, after stabbing it again, he dragged it to a new site for reburial.

Early in September a thirty-one-year-old servant girl named Ida Reuter was raped and battered to death with a hammer. A few days later yet another servant girl, a half-gypsy named Elisabeth Dorrier, suffered the same fate.

In October a housewife, Frau Meurer, was walking home when a 'respectable' man asked her if she was not afraid to be walking out alone so late at night. Before she could reply, he beat her to the ground with a hammer. The same day a prostitute was similarly attacked, but like Frau Meurer, she survived.

It was probably the sheer casual bravado of the attacks which kept Peter Kurten from arrest for so long, for by the end of 1929 he was the world's most

Above left: *Gertrude Schulte survived an attack by Kurten despite being stabbed in the neck several times.*

Above: *Frau Meurer was another who survived a vicious attack by Kurten.*

'I'D RATHER DIE!' SAID THE SHOCKED GIRL WHEN KURTEN BEGGED TO HAVE SEX WITH HER. 'WELL, DIE THEN!' HE REPLIED, STABBING HER

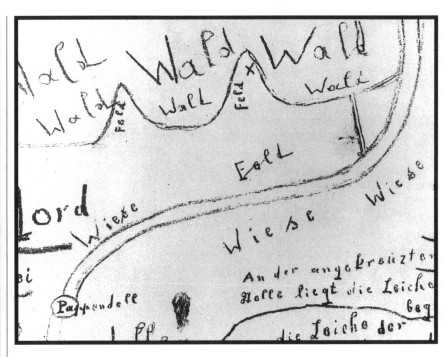

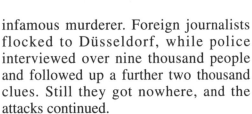

Left: *Peter Kurten, the picture of respectability.*

Above: *The map drawn by Kurten showing where two of his victims were buried.*

infamous murderer. Foreign journalists flocked to Düsseldorf, while police interviewed over nine thousand people and followed up a further two thousand clues. Still they got nowhere, and the attacks continued.

The last murder took place on 7 November, when five-year-old Gertrude Albermann disappeared. Two days later, Kurten wrote to the Communist newspaper *Freiheit* (Freedom). He enclosed a map showing the location of the body, along with a plan of the Pappendale Meadows with the position of another burial site marked.

The police recovered Gertrude's body, strangled and stabbed thirty-five times. At Pappendale they exhumed the body of Maria Hahn. Among the hundreds of sightseers who watched as the police dug was, of course, Peter Kurten.

IDENTIFIED THROUGH A FLUKE

His capture came about by an unlikely chance. On 19 May 1930 a certain Frau Brugmann opened and read a letter which arrived wrongly at her address.

It was from a twenty-year-old servant girl named Maria Budlick who had gone back with a man to his apartment at Mettmannerstrasse.

During the course of the evening he had turned nasty, demanding sex. Frightened, Maria had complied, and the couple had copulated standing up in a doorway. He then led her back to a tram stop and left her to find her way to a convent, where the nuns had given her a bed.

In view of the intense police hunt then going on for a sex maniac, Fraù Brugmann felt she ought to hand this extraordinary letter to the authorities. A Chief Inspector Gennat, who was in charge of the case and was by now clutching at straws, sought out Maria Budlick. In turn, she led the policeman to the address 71 Mettmannerstrasse where the man had taken her, and showed

Gennat the empty room into which she had been led. On the way downstairs she met the man who had raped her. He went pale. Later, the landlady told her that his name was Peter Kurten.

Looking through his files, Gennat found that Kurten had been among the thousands of people interviewed after a woman had accused him of attacking her. So flimsy was the evidence against the respectable tradesman, however, that the police had fined the woman for wasting their time. When questioned, the neighbours assured Gennat that Kurten was a pleasant, likeable man whom children seemed to take to instantly.

Kurten heard of these enquiries and knew instinctively that the game was up. Indeed his behaviour suggests that, like many subsequent serial killers, he had reached a point where his principal urge was to be caught.

On 23 May he told his long-suffering wife that he was the 'monster of Düsseldorf' and had killed even more victims than the police thought – the final estimation was about twenty-two or twenty-three.

Frau Kurten's reaction was of horror and dismay and she suggested a suicide pact. But Kurten had a better idea. There was a large reward offered for the capture of the killer. If his wife could claim that, she could live in comfort. And so on the afternoon of 24 May, outside the St Rochus church and almost by appointment, Peter Kurten was finally arrested.

TEXTBOOK SERIAL KILLER

In prison, he gave a long and highly detailed confession to the police psychiatrist, Dr – later Professor – Karl Berg. He even admitted to setting a number of fatal fires in 1911 and 1912. Peter Kurten's confession was to provide the basis for later analysis into the minds of serial killers.

Most people, of course, were horrified when details of Kurten's career came to light, but many were not. For every letter abusing him which arrived at Düsseldorf jail, there was at least one other which was a love letter or a request for an autograph. Kurten revelled in them all.

His trial opened at Düsseldorf Criminal Court on 13 April 1931 and lasted ten days. His defence was insanity, but after listening to complex psychiatric evidence the jury retired for only ninety minutes before returning a Guilty verdict on nine counts of murder.

Kurten was sentenced to death. His lawyer formally appealed, but the appeal was turned down on 30 June, and the execution was set for 2 July at 6 a.m.

It was to be only two years before Adolf Hitler swept to power, but meanwhile liberalism ran deep in the dying Weimar republic and the death penalty was rarely used. The last condemned man actually to die was a double murderer named Bottcher, executed in Berlin in 1928. The German Humanitarian League protested against the Kurten sentence, and letters of support poured into the prison.

But for a killer of Kurten's notoriety there could be no reprieve – and in any case, the last person to wish for such an outcome was Peter Kurten himself. Execution in Germany was by guillotine, and he was fascinated by the instrument. Would he, he asked Dr Berg, be able – even for an instant – to hear the gushing of his own blood when the blade fell?

Berg said that he thought that this was physiologically possible, and Kurten was delighted. After eating an outsized last 'breakfast' of Wiener schnitzel, fried potatoes and white wine, the monster of Düsseldorf went to his fate smiling and replete.

UNABLE TO FACE BEING A MURDERER'S WIDOW, FRAU KURTEN SUGGESTED A SUICIDE PACT. NO, SAID KURTEN, SHE SHOULD TURN HIM IN AND COLLECT THE REWARD

KURTEN WAS FASCINATED BY THE PROSPECT OF HEARING HIS OWN BLOOD GUSH OUT AS THE GUILLOTINE FELL

Below: *Kurten listening to proceedings during his trial.*

EDWARD GEIN
The Secret Hunter

Warped and perverted by an emotionally disturbed childhood, Edward Gein was to turn his small-town rural community into the centre of a ghoulish murder case – inspiration for *The Silence of the Lambs* and Hitchcock's thriller *Psycho*

The central plain of Wisconsin is one of the most melancholy and uninspiring tracts of land in the United States. It consists of flat, stony farmland about 120 miles square, fit only for raising scrubby cereal crops and equally lean livestock. In the 1950s it was scattered with dilapidated farmsteads clustered around a few small towns.

One of these was Plainfield, which,

Above: *Mary Hogan, one of Gein's victims. She was running a local bar when she disappeared.*

Above right: *Hogan's Tavern, a barn-like saloon, exalts its regulars to drink Blatz Beer.*

Opposite: *Edward Gein, the handyman from Plainfield, Wisconsin, who was charged with mass murder.*

Below: *The farmhouse where Edward Gein lived and killed. Bernice Worden's corpse was found here.*

founded by German settlers in 1849, had grown in a hundred years to accommodate about 800 souls. In an area of clapboard houses and gloomy non-conformist chapels, about the only place of human warmth and interest was Hogan's Tavern, and even that was no stately pleasure-dome.

BLOODSTAINS AT HOGAN'S TAVERN

The tavern was presided over by its eponymous owner, Mary Hogan. She was a big, buxom woman in her early fifties with a broken nose and a colourful past.

She had come to Plainfield before the Second World War from Chicago, where, it was rumoured, she had run a speakeasy and brothel for one of the Prohibition

Above: *Plainfield, Wisconsin was a small farming community. Founded in 1849, its population never reached a thousand.*

DURING THE DEER-HUNTING SEASON CARCASSES WERE DISEMBOWELLED IN THE OPEN AND THE BLOODSTAINED REMAINS ABANDONED IN THE SNOW

mobs. Most of the local menfolk would gather at Hogan's to drink beer and yarn away the long evenings.

On the afternoon of 8 December 1954, a local farmer named Seymour Lester entered the deserted bar room, stamping his boots on the floor and calling for service. There was no reply. Seymour's eye was drawn to a large dark patch on the floor leading into a back room. It was blood, soaking into the pine floorboards.

Seymour scuttled to the telephone and soon Wautoma County Sheriff Harold S. Thompson arrived, followed by a couple of deputies. A search of the premises revealed a .32 calibre rifle cartridge case near the blood patch. Further bloodstains led out through the back door and across the snow to where tyre tracks indicated that a vehicle about the size of a pick-up truck had been parked.

The cash register had not been interfered with, and it seemed to Sheriff Thompson that Mary Hogan had been shot down and spirited away.

UNEXPLAINED DISAPPEARANCES

It was not the first time that the area had experienced sudden disappearances. In May 1947 a schoolgirl from the nearby hamlet of Jefferson had vanished after being given a lift home by a neighbour. In November 1952 Victor 'Bunk' Travis, a Plainfield farmer, set off with his friend Ray Burgess to hunt deer during the Wisconsin open season. Both men subsequently vanished.

Of more interest to the men investigating the Hogan case was the affair of fifteen-year-old Evelyn Hartley, who had apparently been abducted while baby-sitting for a neighbour in November 1953. As in the Hogan disappearance, there were signs of a scuffle and bloodstains had been found leading from the house.

The Travis–Burgess case was perhaps the most explicable. During the nine-day deer-hunting season, tourists flocked in from Milwaukee and Chicago to track their prey through the snowy woodlands of central Wisconsin.

Many of them had little experience of either woodcraft or firearms, and accidents were frequent. In 1957, for instance, thirteen hunting visitors died in the Plainfield area from stray bullets.

At the best of times, the deer-hunting season was not for the squeamish. Hunters 'gralloched' their kill in the open, stringing up the carcasses from

trees, porches or any suitable structure, slitting up their abdomens. Edible portions such as liver, kidneys and hearts would be removed, and the rest of the offal abandoned. The empty husk of the carcase would then be lashed across the radiator of the hunter's truck and driven away for skinning and quartering elsewhere.

One of the few Plainfield farmers to express his disgust at this slaughter was a slightly built bachelor named Edward Theodore Gein.

LOVELESS CHILDHOOD

Gein was descended from the first wave of German settlers, though the two sides of his family were diametrically different in outlook. Edward's father, George Gein, was an orphan who had been brought up on a farm near the township of La Crosse by his god-fearing grandparents. In 1899 he had married. His wife, Augusta, ran the family grocery store in La Crosse.

A strict Lutheran, Augusta soon grew to dread and despise her husband's drinking and violence. Nevertheless the couple had two sons, Henry, born in 1902, and Edward Theodore, born on 27 August 1906.

In 1913 George Gein inherited his grandparents' farm near La Crosse, and the family moved out to work it. A year later they bought a larger spread just outside Plainfield. George Gein died of alcoholic excess in 1940, aged sixty-six, and was buried in the Plainfield cemetery.

George had given love to no one. Augusta seemed incapable of doing so. Instead of affection, she showered scriptural texts on her sons, reminding

Above: Gein used Bernice Worden's own pick-up to move her body.

Below: Sheriff Art Schley. The Gein investigation was his first murder case.

them constantly that they were sinners.

Henry seemed able to detach himself from his mother's hide-bound views, but his brother Edward grew morose and solitary.

In the spring of 1944, Henry and Eddie Gein suffered a brush fire on their farm and were separated by the smoke. Eddie ran for help, and managed to lead a search party directly to where his brother lay dead. Henry had bruising to his forehead, but an autopsy gave the cause of death as smoke inhalation.

LONE SURVIVOR

Shortly after Henry's death, Augusta suffered a stroke. For twelve months Eddie nursed her tenderly back to what seemed like full health, but in December 1945 she suddenly collapsed and died. Eddie was left by himself in the big old 'L'-shaped timber farmhouse, with its annexe at the rear which he called his 'summer kitchen'.

He was known as a hard-working and honest man, but was not talkative. Unlike his father Eddie was never a heavy drinker, though he enjoyed the odd evening sitting over a beer or two down at Hogan's Tavern, and seemed to miss Mary Hogan when she was gone.

This point was made to Eddie one morning by Elmo Ueeck, who owned the Plainfield sawmill, when Eddie was over at the mill fixing fences some weeks after Mary's disappearance. If Eddie had taken a shine to Mary Hogan, Ueeck teased, why hadn't he said so when she was still around? Then maybe she would have been back at Gein's farm cooking supper for him, instead of being missing and maybe lying dead somewhere.

Gein, Ueeck was to recall later, rolled his eyes and shifted his weight from foot to foot, before giving one of his strange, tooth-baring, lopsided grins. 'She ain't missing,' he said after some deliberation. 'She's at the farm right now.'

Elmo Ueeck thought no more about Eddie's odd fancy. It was just the sort of strange remark he would make.

DEATH AT THE HARDWARE STORE

Three years went by, and the time of the annual deer cull approached again. One woman who always looked forward to the increased trade was Bernice Worden. A plump and homely widow in her late fifties, she ran Worden's Hardware and Implement Store, selling everything from agricultural tools to ammunition.

Bernice was now preparing to hand over the store to her son, Frank, who served as deputy sheriff of Plainfield, and settle down to enjoy her retirement in the company of her grandchildren.

Recently, Bernice had been vaguely troubled by the presence of Eddie Gein. For the last few weeks he had taken to sitting in his pick-up outside the store, or standing opposite, gazing across at her.

On Friday, 15 November 1957, just before she closed for the night, Gein had wandered in, looked around vaguely and asked her the price of anti-freeze. When she told him he wandered off again without a word.

Saturday, 16 November, was the first day of the deer-hunting season. When dawn broke, the town emptied of its menfolk as they made for the woods in their pick-up trucks, rifles racked behind them. Only one customer appeared at Worden's store as Bernice opened up at 8.30a.m.: Eddie Gein.

This time Eddie had an empty half-

Above: Edward Gein adored his dominant mother. He professed to hating violence in any form.

'SHE AIN'T MISSING,' SAID EDDIE OF THE MURDERED MARY. 'SHE'S AT THE FARM RIGHT NOW'

Below: Police found Mary Hogan's face and scalp behind rubbish stacked in Gein's summer house.

gallon jug, which he asked Bernice to fill with anti-freeze. He paid for it and left by the back door, while Bernice returned to the front of the store to fill out a sales slip with Eddie's name and purchase.

At this point, according to Eddie's later testimony, he walked back in, picked up a hunting rifle and, while pretending to admire it, loaded it and shot Bernice. He then dragged her out to her own pick-up truck and drove off with her body.

Bernard Muschinski, who managed the filling station just down and across the street from Worden's store, looked out of his office at 8.45a.m. and saw Bernice's pick-up truck pull out from the store's back yard and roar away. At lunchtime he walked past the store and was surprised to see that the lights were still on, though the door was locked. Bernice he guessed was growing forgetful.

In mid-morning, Elmo Ueeck had caught sight of Eddie Gein in slightly embarrassing circumstances. The sawmill owner had chased a deer off his own property and on to Eddie's, where he had managed to shoot it.

He had brought his truck round on to Eddie's land to whisk the carcass away, when he saw Eddie's old Ford sedan bouncing down the rutted track towards him. Eddie clearly saw the dead deer tied across Ueeck's front fender, but merely gave a friendly wave and roared past in a flurry of frozen slush. At lunchtime he drove back to apologize, but Eddie

cheerfully waved away Elmo Ueeck's explanation.

That afternoon Bob Hill and his sister Darlene, Eddie's cousins, walked across to see him. They wanted him to run them into town to pick up a new car battery, as theirs had gone flat.

Gein stepped out briskly on to the porch to greet them. He was in his shirtsleeves and, to their surprise, his hands and arms were dappled with blood.

Bob knew of Gein's often expressed horror of blood and butchery, but his cousin seemed calm as he told them he had been dressing a deer. After going indoors to wash his hands, he came out and drove them into Plainfield. When he drove them back home, their mother, Irene, invited him to stay for supper.

Meanwhile, Frank Worden had called at Bernard Muschinski's gas station to fill up his car. There he heard that his mother's store was still locked, though the lights were on.

Frank opened the door with a spare key and viewed the scene with a sinking heart. There was a large patch of blood on the floor, and the cash register had been torn from its screws on the counter.

He rang the new sheriff of Wautoma County, thirty-two-year-old Art Schley, and then set about searching the store. By the time Schley arrived, Frank had found his mother's last sales slip. It had Gein's name on it.

'He's done something to her,' Worden told the sheriff and his deputy.

'Who?' the sheriff asked.

Worden held out the docket. 'Ed Gein,' he said. Sheriff Schley put out a radio call for Gein to be brought in, as news of the dramatic and not unprecedented events spread around the town.

Up at the Hills' farm, Eddie Gein was just finishing his supper when a neighbour called by with the news of the disappearance.

'It must have been somebody pretty cold-blooded,' commented Eddie.

Irene Hill turned to her cousin. 'How come,' she asked jocularly, 'that every time someone gets banged on the head and hauled away, you're always around?'

In reply, she was to remember, Gein shrugged his shoulders and grinned his toothy grin.

Bob Hill suggested that he and Eddie should drive into town to see what was going on. Gein cheerfully agreed, but as the two men stepped across the freezing, starlit yard a police squad car skidded to a stop. Traffic Officer Dan Chase and

A WOMAN'S BODY WAS HANGING BY ITS HEELS FROM THE RAFTERS – SHE HAD BEEN BEHEADED AND DISEMBOWELLED JUST LIKE A DEER

Deputy 'Poke' Spees got out, and Gein was taken in for questioning.

On the way into town, Chase asked him what he had been doing that day. Gein told him. Questioned on details, however, Gein became muddled, and then said: 'Somebody framed me.'

'Framed you for what?' Chased asked.

'Well, about Mrs Worden,' Gein replied. 'She's dead, ain't she? I heard it. They told me in there.'

SECRETS OF THE 'SUMMER KITCHEN'

With Gein in custody, Sheriff Schley called in a more experienced colleague, Captain Lloyd Schoephoerster of the nearby Green Lake County Sheriff's office. Together they drove to Gein's farmhouse. The yard was dark and deserted as the headlights of their car illuminated the dark wooden walls of Gein's 'summer kitchen'.

Flashlights in hand, the two men walked up the steps and pushed open the creaking door. As he entered the room, Art Schley felt something brush his shoulder. He whirled around. The beam of his torch fell on the bloody stump of a human neck. It belonged to the naked torso of a stout woman, hanging by the tendons of her heels from the rafters. She had been beheaded and cleanly disembowelled – 'gralloched' like a deer.

When the two officers had radioed for reinforcements, they ventured back into the house. They could find no lights, and until a mobile generator was rigged they and their helpers searched by torchlight.

It was a cesspit, a rotting rubbish dump of old metal and organic remains. Apart from the grisly corpse hanging from the ceiling there were piles of old clothes, dirty pans and dishes, broken chairs, dusty packages of half-eaten, mouldering food, and heaps of gaudy-covered magazines.

These proved to be a mixture of garish horror comics which dealt with stories of torture and flagellation, war crimes and 'true' detective magazines, and more or less 'straight' pornography. The kitchen sink was filled with sand, and there was a sinister, grinning row of dentures on the mantlepiece.

The full horror of the scene was only revealed when the generator was rigged. As the powerful light chased shadows away, it shone in the eye sockets of a number of skulls. Some lay tumbled under the table, others had been sawn in half and were apparently used as bowls. Two of them were impaled on the posts of a rag- and fur-strewn bed in which Gein presumably slept.

Then came the skin. As forensic scientists arrived and poked around in the growing dawn, they realized that a kitchen chair had a seat of human hide. Soon they had turned up lampshades, the sheath of a hunting knife, a drum, a bracelet and a wastepaper basket – all made from crudely tanned human skin.

There was a skin shirt, the pendulous dried breasts still attached, clearly made from the top half of a woman's body, and several pairs of human skin 'leggings'. And in cardboard boxes were bones and pieces of dried flesh, the debris of this ghoulish tannery.

But the biggest shocks were still to come, for Eddie Gein had a collection of 'shrunken heads'. They hung on the walls of his bedroom, some by their hair, some from hooks thrust through their ears. Gein had obviously peeled the flesh away from the skulls and stuffed the resulting faces and scalps with old rags and newspapers. All seemed, by the length of the hair, to be women's faces. One bore the still recognizable features of Mary Hogan.

By now the heat of the arc lamps had made the stench almost unbearable, despite the freezing weather outside. But the searchers had a few more vital items to discover. They finally found them in and around the cold and rusted kitchen stove.

Bernice Worden's heart was in a plastic bag and the rest of her entrails lay nearby, wrapped in an old coat. In a meal bag lay her head, bloodied around the nostrils but with a strangely peaceful expression on her face. Her ears, however, had already been pierced with hanging hooks...

Less dramatic, but still surprising, was the main part of the house. This, locked and boarded off from the chamber of horrors at the rear, proved to be a perfectly ordinary, though dust-covered,

THE HORRIFIED POLICE REALIZED THAT GEIN'S CLOTHING, FURNITURE AND HOUSEHOLD EFFECTS HAD ALL BEEN FASHIONED FROM HUMAN SKIN

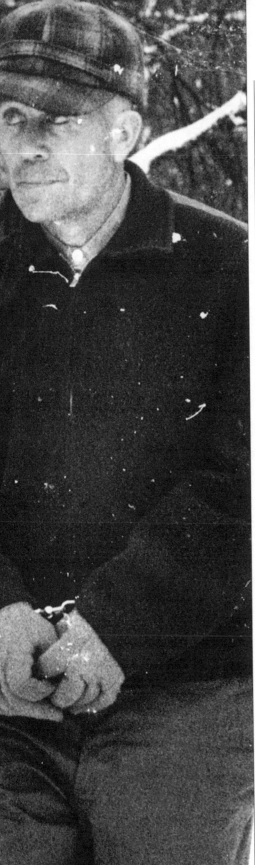

family home. It was a shrine to Augusta Gein, untouched and unseen by outside eyes since her death over a decade previously.

During the morning of Sunday, 17 November, the human relics from Gein's hellish kitchen were bagged and tagged and despatched to Gault's Funeral Home for post-mortem examination. Gein, meanwhile, sat silently in the town's jailhouse, his stubbled jaw hanging and his eyes rolling damply.

For twelve hours he uttered not a word, even when Sheriff Schley, fresh from the mayhem of the ranch, lost control and struck him. During the afternoon, however, an initial autopsy showed that Bernice Worden had been shot in the head with a .22 bullet.

NEED FOR HUMAN REMAINS

On 18 November, Monday morning, Gein slowly began to reply to the questioning of the local District Attorney, Earl Kileen. He confessed to having shot Mrs Worden and loaded her body into her own pick-up truck, along with the cash register which, he said, he wanted to 'strip down to see how it worked'.

After dumping the pick-up in the woods near his home, he had transferred the body to his Ford sedan and strung it up with a sharpened branch through the ankle tendons. He had bled the corpse into a bucket, afterwards burying the fresh blood in the ground. Asked by Kileen if he thought he had been dressing a deer, he replied, 'That is the only explanation I can think of.'

Mrs Worden, he claimed, was the only person he ever remembered killing, but during the past few years he had felt the need for human remains. Sometimes he watched the newspapers for the funerals of people he knew had died, and then went to the graveyard and stole the corpses. He always, he claimed, 'then left the graves in apple-pie order'.

Which neatly introduced a topic that had preyed on Kileen's mind. Had Gein ever eaten any parts of the corpses?

The farmer looked genuinely horrified, and vigorously shook his head.

Had he then ever had sexual relations with any of them?

'No! No!' replied Gein. 'In any case, they smelt too bad.'

That afternoon Gein was held on a charge of armed robbery – stealing the cash register – and then spent the rest of the day helping the police with their enquiries.

Left: *November 1957 – Edward Gein stands handcuffed on the farmland where human remains were discovered.*

He pointed out the spot where he had poured away Bernice Worden's blood. Later he was interviewed about the four-year mystery of the disappearance of Evelyn Hartley, the fifteen-year-old baby sitter. Gein seemed never to have heard of her.

When questioned about Mary Hogan, however, whose head had been found on his premises, Gein lapsed into silence again. Then, in a faltering voice, he admitted that he had 'called into her bar for a drink, once or twice'.

The following day, Tuesday, the hoard of pressmen which had converged on Plainfield and had been filing wildly speculative stories ever since, was finally allowed up to Gein's property. Sheriff Schley promptly got into a fist fight with a number of reporters.

Gein was taken to the State Central Crime Laboratory in the state capital, Madison, for lie detector tests. Strapped to the equipment for almost nine hours, Eddie Gein readily admitted to making and wearing the 'garments' of human skin, and said that he thought that he 'may have murdered Mary Hogan, but was very hazy' about it.

On the subject of Bernice Worden, however, he claimed that this was an accident. He was to keep up the protest for the remainder of his life.

On Thursday, 21 November, Gein was formally charged with the first degree murders of Worden and Hogan. His attorney entered a plea of insanity, and the judge committed the accused to the Central State Hospital for the Criminally Insane in Waupun, pending psychological tests.

By now, DA Kileen had obtained from Gein a list of the persons whose graves he remembered robbing, and the focus of interest moved to Plainfield Town Cemetery. Pat Danna, the sexton, claimed that none of the graves had been disturbed, but the exhumation party chose to examine the tomb of Mrs Eleanor Adams – who was, coincidentally, buried a few feet from Gein's parents. (Later it was explained that, had he tried to disturb his own mother, he would have to break into a concrete vault to get at her.)

As the frozen soil was scraped away

Above: Gein was incarcerated in Mendota Mental Health Institute, a gothic pile near Madison, Wisconsin.

Right: Sheriff Art Schley steers Edward Gein into the Central State Hospital at Waupun, Wisconsin.

GEIN WAS APPALLED WHEN THE DISTRICT ATTORNEY ASKED IF HE HAD EVER EATEN CORPSES OR MADE LOVE TO THEM

from Mrs Adams's casket, the lid was seen to be split in two. The coffin itself proved to be empty except for rotting bits of burial shroud and a 12-inch steel crowbar.

Digging continued at Gein's farm. In a rubbish dump, the near complete skeleton of a woman with a gold tooth was discovered. In another burial trench a jumbled mass of bones had been interred.

After further lie detector and psychological tests, forensic scientist Joe Wilimovski became convinced that Gein had killed only Hogan and Worden, and had otherwise confined his hobby of mutilation to the bodies of already dead women. Nine corpses had by now been assembled from the unidentified portions, all of them middle-aged women.

During his questioning, Gein spoke calmly and apparently rationally about the dismemberments and flayings. He seemed to find little wrong with what he had done, and was apparently rather proud of his unsuspected anatomical knowledge.

The standard Wechsler adult intelligence test showed that Eddie Gein was 'quite bright' and in some ways above average, except for his almost total inability to communicate with other people in any but the most basic terms.

Psychologists at the hospital put this down to a 'severe emotional disturbance' in his early development. This had retarded his normal sexual-emotional development causing him to retreat into a bizarre fantasy world in which his sexual urges became confused by grief over the death of his mother, combined with fear of transgressing the strait-laced moral code she had imbued in him while she was alive.

As one expert, Dr Milton Miller, put it: 'In many ways, the patient has lived a psychotic life for years. He has substituted human parts for the companionship of human beings.'

On 6 January 1958, as Eddie Gein sat blankly chewing gum, Circuit Judge Herbert Bunde briefly heard the comments of three psychologists and committed him indefinitely to the state hospital. Almost three months later Gein's farm, which was due to be put up for auction, was mysteriously consumed by fire while many of Plainfield's leading citizens – including Deputy Sheriff Frank Worden – looked on. Gein's comment was: 'Just as well.'

As the Gein case unfolded, Robert Bloch, a writer living in Weyauwega, 30 miles east of Plainfield, followed it with interest. He was intrigued by the psychologists' report that the influence of a long-dead mother could drive a man to commit such strange and inhuman crimes.

But, like other Mid-West dwellers, he was even more astonished that 'a ghoulish killer with perverted sexual appetites could flourish almost openly in a small rural community where everybody prides himself on knowing everyone else's business'.

Bloch's resulting novel *Psycho* was filmed by Alfred Hitchcock in 1960. And nearly thirty years later another novel-based film, *The Silence of the Lambs*, which featured a man who made suits out of female skin, also echoed the bizarre doings at Plainfield.

In January 1968, District Judge Robert Gollmar heard from the hospital authorities that their patient was now deemed sufficiently sane to stand trial, and Eddie Gein was marched into the dock. It was a short-lived appearance. Eddie was found guilty but insane, and returned to hospital.

There, despite being a model inmate, he was to remain for the rest of his life. He died in the geriatrics wing of Mendota Mental Health Institute on 26 July 1984, and was buried in an unmarked grave at Plainfield, beside his mother.

ONE NIGHT THE FARM BURNT DOWN, WATCHED BY PROMINENT PLAINFIELD CITIZENS. 'JUST AS WELL,' WAS GEIN'S COMMENT FROM THE MENTAL HOSPITAL

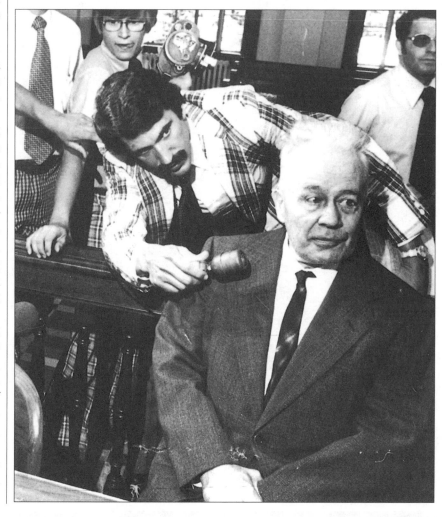

Below: *Edward Gein awaits the start of his unsuccessful petition for release from Central State Hospital in 1974.*

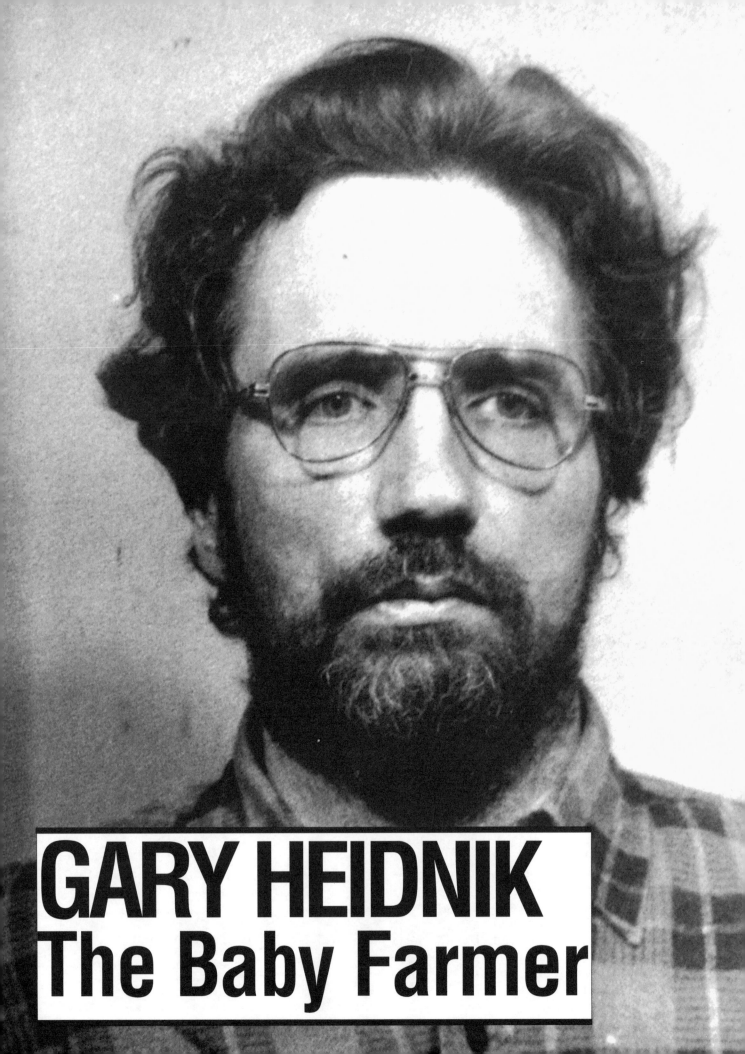

GARY HEIDNIK
The Baby Farmer

Gary Heidnik believed God wanted him to people the world. So he kidnapped women to start his 'baby farm', feeding them on dog food and human flesh. Was he insane, or, as the judge said at his trial, merely 'possessed of a malignancy in his heart'?

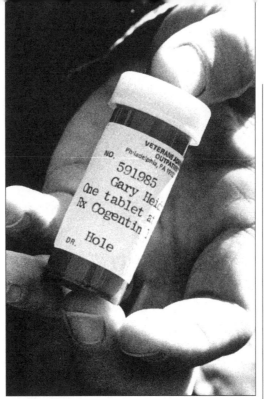

Left: *Medicine prescribed for Heidnik by Dr Hole.*

Opposite: *Gary Heidnik believed that he had a divine calling to procreate. He kidnapped women and started his 'baby farm'.*

On the freezing cold night of 24 March 1987, Philadelphia police received a telephone call from a box in the neighbourhood of Sixth and Girard Streets. The caller, who identified himself as Vincent Nelson, was excited but apologetic, as if he found the story he had to tell difficult to believe.

His ex-girlfriend, Josefina Riviera, a half-black, half-Puerto Rican prostitute, had turned up at his house after a long absence. 'She was...you know...talking real fast about this guy having three girls

Below: *Josefina Riviera (right) leaves court with another of Hednik's victims, having given evidence at his trial.*

'SHE SAID THAT HE WAS BEATING THEM UP, RAPING THEM, HAD THEM EATING DEAD PEOPLE...'

chained up in the basement of this house and she was held hostage for four months....She said that he was beating them up, raping them, had them eating dead people just like he was a cold blooded nut....I thought she was crazy.'

HORROR IN THE BASEMENT

The police switchboard operator was inclined, on the evidence, to side with the latter point of view. Nevertheless he despatched a patrol car. Officers David Savidge and John Cannon picked up Nelson and the distressed Josefina and took them to the precinct house.

There, a brief examination of Josefina's skinny body convinced the police that something untoward had happened to her. Her ankles, in particular, bore the marks where shackles had eroded the flesh.

She managed to tell them that her captor was named Gary Heidnik, and that he was due to pick her up in his new grey and white Cadillac Coupe de Ville, with his initials 'GMH' on the door, at the gas station on Sixth and Girard.

Officers Savidge and Cannon cruised around to the filling station. There, sure enough, was the Cadillac. The driver was a greasy-haired man with cold blue eyes, dressed in a fringed buckskin jacket and gaudy shirt. After admitting that he was Gary Heidnik, he was taken to the Philadelphia Police Department Sex Crimes Unit for further questioning.

At 4.30a.m. on 25 March, a squad of officers bearing a search warrant, crowbars and a sledge hammer arrived at Heidnik's address – 3520 North Marshall Street.

The foetid stench hit them as they broke the locks of the door. Following

Below: *Searching for evidence of Heidnik's crimes in the basement of his house.*

two evils. In an aluminium pot were boiled human ribs, while the fridge contained a jointed human arm. Officer Savidge, hardened as he was, had to run outside for air.

Back at the precinct house, Josefina Riviera slowly began to piece together a statement. She explained that Gary had a notion of starting a 'baby farm' in his basement. A religious freak, he claimed that God had commanded him to collect women so that, 'like a bee to flowers', he could move from one naked woman to another, impregnating them.

Josefina herself was twenty-five years old and had been brought up in an orphanage by nuns. Since her early teens she had worked the streets as a prostitute.

On 26 November 1986 Josefina met Gary Heidnik for the first time. Heidnik took her to a McDonald's where he had a coffee, ignoring Josefina. Finally he suggested they go back to his house in North Marshall Street.

As he parked in the garage she noticed a 1971 Rolls Royce, and in the house itself the hallway was papered with $1 and $5 bills. But again, these signs of opulence were spoilt by the squalor of the bedroom, which contained only two battered chairs, a table and a big waterbed.

The pair then stripped, and the sex act was over in minutes. Gary handed her a $20 bill, and Josefina reached for her jeans. Then her nightmare began.

THE 'BABY FARM'

Heidnik leaped from the bed, grabbed her wrists and handcuffed her. Before she realized what was happening he dragged her out and down several flights of stairs to a dim and filthy cellar, lit only by narrow windows set near the ceiling. Metal heating pipes ran around the room, and he shackled her ankle to one of these, using a U-shaped link and a length of chain. Then he slapped her down on to an evil-smelling mattress, placed his head in her naked lap, told her to be quiet and slept. Josefina noticed a shallow pit in the centre of the room. This, covered by boards, was to be used by Heidnik as a 'punishment pit'.

Three days later Heidnik went out again. He was looking for his former

Josefina's instructions they made their way down to the basement, where their torches picked out the terrified faces of two black women huddled under a blanket on a dirty mattress. The women were shackled, chained, filthy and naked apart from skimpy vests, and they cringed and whimpered in the light.

When they were calmer, they indicated a shallow pit in the floor. In it was another black woman, naked and with her hands handcuffed behind her back.

But when the officers examined the kitchen, they began to believe that starvation would have been the lesser of

Above: Police sift through the debris in Heidnik's house.

APPALLED AT THE FILTHY, EMACIATED WOMEN, THE OFFICERS HAD WORSE TO COME WHEN THEY EXAMINED THE CONTENTS OF THE KITCHEN

Above: *Heidnik believed he was carrying out God's will.*

TO PUNISH SANDRA LINDSAY HEIDNIK HUNG HER FROM A BEAM AND FORCE-FED HER BREAD UNTIL SHE CHOKED AND DIED

were lured back to join Heidnik's 'baby farm'. Lisa Thomas, aged nineteen, was picked up on 22 December. On New Year's Day 1987, twenty-three-year-old Deborah Dudley became his fourth victim, while his fifth and youngest, nineteen-year-old Jacquelyn Askins joined the unwilling harem on 18 January. Another girl, Agnes Adams, known on the streets as 'Vickie', was tricked by Gary Heidnik into going back with him through her acquaintance with Josefina. She arrived the day before the latter's escape.

Every day, Heidnik beat the girls and forced them to perform sexual acts with both him and each other. He fed them a curious diet of bread, dog food and ice cream, which he kept in a deep freeze in the corner of the cellar. Later, another ingredient was to be added.

At some time during the New Year Sandra Lindsay annoyed Heidnik. To punish her, he strapped her by one wrist to an overhead beam and then forced her to eat lumps of bread, holding her lips together until she swallowed. For a week the half-witted girl dangled feverishly from the beam, until finally she choked on a piece of bread and died.

He carried the body upstairs. Soon the girls in the cellar heard the whine of an electric saw, followed by the pungent odour of cooking flesh.

That night Deborah Dudley had a bout of rebelliousness, and physically fought Heidnik when he tried to force himself upon her. In reply, the furious man unshackled her and dragged her upstairs.

A few minutes later she came down, silent and shocked. When she could speak, she told the others: 'He showed me Sandra's head in a pot. And he had her ribs in a roasting pan, and a bunch of her other body parts in the freezer. He told me if I didn't start listening to him, that was going to happen to me too.'

But despite the horror of what she had seen, Deborah rebelled again. This time she was thrust down into the pit in the floor, and water was poured in on top of her. Then Heidnik made Josefina push a live electric wire through a hole in the boards covering the pit. Deborah gave one terrible scream. When the boards were removed, she lay dead in the water.

lover, a slightly retarded black girl of twenty-five named Sandra Lindsay. Some time before, Heidnik was to explain to Josefina, he had paid Sandra $1000 to have his baby but she had aborted it.

That evening he came back with the terrified Sandra, and she too was stripped and shackled. The women, forced to perform various sexual acts, were told by Heidnik that they were the nucleus of his 'baby farm'.

The following day the two girls had a moment of hope when they heard pounding on the front door. Gary told them later that the callers had been Sandra's sister, Teresa, and two cousins, searching for her in her old haunts.

Over the next few weeks, more women

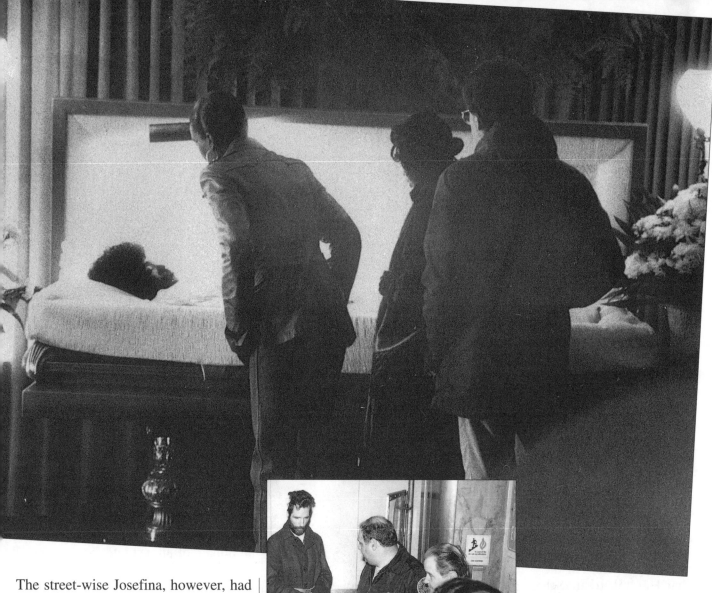

Above: *The viewing of Deborah Dudley's body.*

Left: *Heidnik being brought into the sheriff's office after his arrest.*

The street-wise Josefina, however, had a streak of cunning. Gradually she worked at winning Heidnik's trust, until he began taking her out on little expeditions to McDonald's and even buying her clothes and wigs. Finally, she begged him to let her see her three children who, she claimed, she had left with a babysitter. Instead she ran to her old boyfriend, Vincent Nelson.

What kind of a monster had the Philadelphia police netted?

BACKGROUND OF A MANIAC

Gary Michael Heidnik had been born on 21 November 1943 in the suburb of Eastlake in Cleveland, Ohio.

At the age of thirteen he became fascinated with things military – he had been a keen Boy Scout – and with his father's profound approval enrolled at the Staunton Military Academy in Virginia. There he scored consistently high marks until, quite suddenly, he dropped out.

In October 1961, as soon as he was old enough, Gary Heidnik joined the US Army. After basic training he was transferred to Landsthul in Germany.

Less than a year later he developed nausea, dizzy spells, headaches and blurred vision. Doctors noticed a series of nervous tics, including sudden head spasms, and he developed a habit of saluting in an exaggeratedly smart fashion at inappropriate moments.

Despite recording his IQ as up to 148 – a 'near genius' level – the army psychiatrists could do little to help Gary out of the slough into which he had fallen. In January 1963 he was given an

US ARMY PSYCHIATRISTS FAILED TO DEAL WITH HEIDNIK'S DEPRESSION OR TO NOTICE HIS EXCESSIVE SEX DRIVE

honourable discharge and, with it, a pension of almost $2000 a month.

Neither the Army nor his civilian psychiatrists noticed Gary Heidnik's extraordinary sexual drive. Even in his forties, shortly before his arrest, he was regularly having sex four times a day, and he spent a great deal of money on prostitutes and sex videos. His only other material interest was in cars.

After his discharge from the army, what friends he had were invariably black. The prostitutes he consorted with were also black, and with rare exceptions, like Josefina Riviera, simple-minded. And it was among these women that he looked for mothers – the mothers of his children.

His obsession that God wanted him to father children led Heidnik, on 12 October 1971, to start a religion to be known as the United Church of the Ministers of God. Gary was the Church's 'Bishop', and his brother Terry a member of the board. The church was registered with the state, and under US law was exempt from taxes.

The congregation was largely comprised of black physical and/or mental cripples. All the evidence shows that Heidnik treated these people with generosity and kindness.

In 1977 he impregnated an illiterate

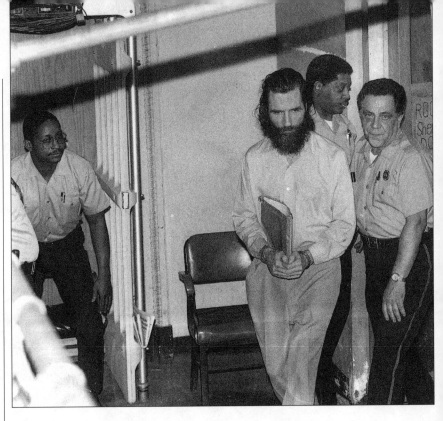

Above: *Heidnik is led into court for his trial at city hall in Philadelphia.*

Below: *The formal charges against Heidnik were all-encompassing.*

black girl named Aljeanette Davidson. She had an IQ of 49, and was completely under Heidnik's thrall. The baby girl was immediately fostered by the state.

Undeterred, Heidnik hatched a wicked plan. Aljeanette's sister, Alberta, was thirty-five and had for twenty years been an inmate of an institute for the mentally handicapped in Harrisburg, Pennsylvania. Gary took Aljeanette to see Alberta, and the elder sister was delighted when her sister's kindly boyfriend suggested they go for 'an outing'.

Alberta failed to return, and the institute officials became worried. Days later the hospital authorities, accompanied by police, broke into the house in North Marshall Street and found the wretched Alberta crammed into a garbage bin in the cellar.

Because she was not deemed fit to give evidence, Heidnik could only be tried on the comparatively trivial charges of assault and abduction. But Judge Charles Mariarchi spotted something 'evil and dangerous' about Heidnik.

Heidnik spent most of the sentence in mental hospitals. For at least six years after his release from jail, Gary Heidnik vanished from all official records except those of the stock market. When he registered his Church in 1971 its total assets were $1500, but twelve years later, despite its founder's curious habits, the funds had multiplied to $545, 000.

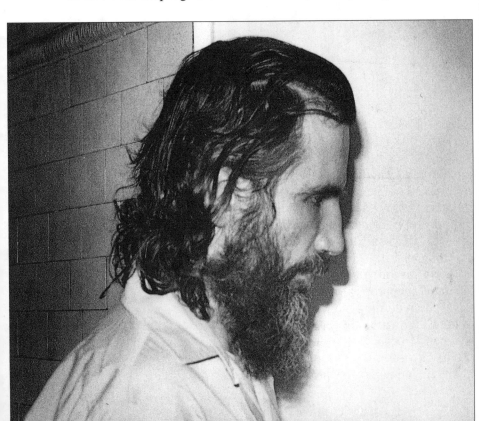

Above: *Friends and relatives of the victims hurry from the courtroom after the jury finally returned their verdict of guilty on all charges.*

TRIAL BY JURY

His trial opened at City Hall, Philadelphia, on 20 June 1988 before Judge Lynne M. Abrahams. The charges against Heidnik were murder, kidnapping, rape, aggravated assault, involuntary deviate sexual intercourse, indecent exposure, false imprisonment, unlawful restraint, simple assault, making terroristic threats, recklessly endangering another person, indecent assault, criminal solicitation, possession, and abuse of a corpse. The judge proved very dubious of arguments presenting Heidnik's acts as 'excusable' because of his alleged mental sickness.

In a three-hour stint in the witness box, Josefina Riviera told how Heidnik had set up his basement baby farm 'because the city was always taking his babies away'. She described in graphic detail the horrors of life in the Heidnik basement.

Food consisted of crackers, oatmeal, chicken, ice-cream, bread, water, and – after the murder of Lindsay – dog food 'mixed with minced body parts'. Very occasionally, their captor would take one of the girls upstairs for a bath, have sex with her, and then bring her down again.

The tiny figure of Jacquelyn Askins presented the most forlorn figure on the witness stand. She was so small that Heidnik had used handcuffs to shackle her ankles, and his lawyers tried to suggest that a degree of compassion had been shown in the extra length of chain he had used to link them. 'Oh no,' said Jacquelyn, 'he did that so I could open my legs for sex.'

After two and a half days the jury brought in a verdict of Guilty on all counts. Heidnik was sentenced to death on two charges – the death penalty was in abeyance in Pennsylvania – and a total of 120 years' imprisonment on the rest.

He was, said Judge Abrahams, possessed 'not of an illness in his head, but a malignancy in his heart. I don't want any parole order to put Mr Heidnik back on the streets as long as he's breathing,' she concluded.

In January 1990 the State Supreme Court refused Heidnik's request to be executed, and almost simultaneously the US Bankruptcy Court divided his $600,000 among his creditors. Each of his surviving victims was awarded $34,540 for her bizarre ordeal.

DID THE LONGER CHAIN ON ASKINS'S ANKLES IMPLY COMPASSION ON HEIDNIK'S PART? NO, SHE REPLIED, IT WAS TO ENABLE SEX TO TAKE PLACE

ED KEMPER
The Headhunter

He started with family pets. Then he moved on to assorted hitch-hikers, his grandmother and mother, carving up the bodies to prevent detection.
Ed Kemper was a paranoid schizophrenic with a John Wayne macho fixation, and he was loose in California

S omeone, in a state so conscious of psychiatry, psychotherapy and general mental maintainance as California, should have spotted Ed Kemper sooner. He started young enough, after all.

When he was nine years old, Ed buried the family cat alive in the back yard. Later he dug up its body, cut off its head, stuck it on a pole and, taking the strange totem to his bedroom, prayed to it.

In 1961, when he was thirteen and in summer camp, Ed was taught to shoot. He celebrated by shooting dead a

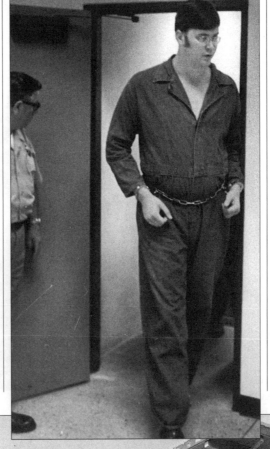

Left: Kemper arriving at court.

Opposite: Edmund Emil Kemper III, the six-foot-nine giant who loved killing things.

ALL HIS LIFE ED KEMPER BELIEVED HE BEHAVED REASONABLY SO LONG AS NO ONE CROSSED HIM — AND THE SIAMESE CAT HAD CROSSED HIM

Below: 609A Ord Drive in Aptos, California was the Kempers' comfortable lower-middle-class home.

classmate's pet dog. But instead of it giving him a macho image – his hero John Wayne was fast with a gun, but always popular – Kemper was reviled for the deed.

Shortly afterwards he wreaked revenge on the new family pet, a Siamese cat. This time he sliced off the top of the animal's skull with a machete, and then stabbed the body. Parts of the cat were hidden in his bedroom cupboard.

BIZARRE BACKGROUND

But if Ed was odd, his family were at least partly to blame.

Ed – Edmund Emil Kemper III, known at home as 'Guy' – was the only son of an ex-Marine who had served with the Special Forces Unit in Europe during the Second World War. Ed III was born on 18 December 1948, and worshipped his 6 ft 8 ins tall father.

In 1957 the father, who despite his size tended to be dominated by Ed's mother Clarnell, left his wife and three young children for another woman. Clarnell sold the family home in California, and moved to Helena, Montana.

Clarnell Kemper herself stood over 6 ft tall, and was a hard drinker. When Ed mourned the departure of his father, his mother feared that he was 'going soft' and might develop into a homosexual. To pre-empt this, she made him sleep in the cellar, locking him in and placing the kitchen table over the trapdoor.

In the summer of 1964, Ed's father felt that the boy needed a complete change. The answer seemed to be his own parents, Edmund and Maude Kemper.

Edmund Kemper I was a quiet, rather colourless man who had worked most of his life for the California State Division of Highways. Now, at seventy-one, he lived in retirement on his smallholding in the foothills of the Sierra Nevada. His wife Maude, sixty-five, was an entirely different creature. Everything and everyone within her sphere of influence was controlled with an iron hand.

On 8 August 1964, Maude's grandson Ed III arrived at the ranch. Maude took against her grandson from the outset. She had to suffer him, in the event, for just sixteen days.

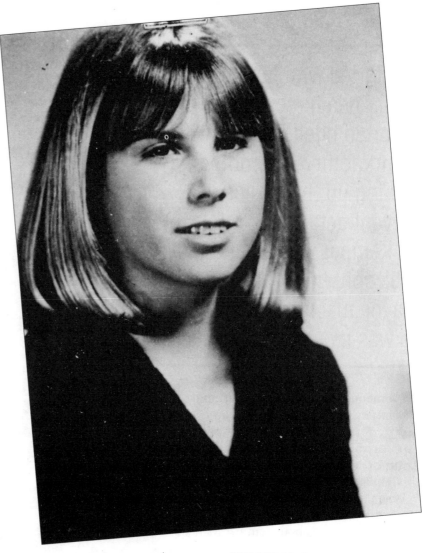

Above: *Anita Luchessa was eighteen and in her first year at Fresno State University when she made the fatal error of accepting a lift from Ed Kemper.*

TO PRE-EMPT ANY 'SOFTNESS' OR HOMOSEXUAL TENDENCIES ED'S MOTHER MADE HIM SLEEP LOCKED UP IN THE CELLAR

SHOOTING GRANDMA

On the hot, airless morning of 27 August 1964, old Ed Kemper set out to fetch the shopping while Maude settled to her typewriter at the kitchen table. Young Ed shuffled around listlessly in the yard for a while, then came in and took his grandfather's .22 rifle from the kitchen door. Loading it, he told his grandmother he was going out to shoot rabbits.

'Just don't shoot any birds,' she snapped. Young Kemper stopped on the threshold. Something about her tone induced an instant surge of white-hot rage. Whipping around he flung the rifle up to his shoulder and fired a shot into the back of her head. As she fell forward he loosed off two more into her back. Then he put down the gun, selected a sharp kitchen knife, and stabbed her repeatedly until his fury drained away.

Then he wrapped a towel around the dead woman's head to soak up the blood, and carried her body into the bedroom.

He realized that he was in trouble. As his grandfather drove up outside, Kemper killed him with a single shot to the head in order, he said later, to spare him the sight of his murdered wife.

After a desultory attempt to clean up the kitchen, Ed rang his mother Clarnell for help. 'There's been an accident,' he said. 'Grandma's dead. So is Grandpa.'

Clarnell, who immediately suspected that her son was responsible, told him to ring the local sheriff. When the lawman arrived, Ed admitted what he had done.

After a session with a court psychiatrist, Ed Kemper was pronounced a paranoid schizophrenic. Without much further examination, it was decided to send him to the State Hospital at Atascadero.

BAD INFLUENCE

The boy murderer was to stay at Atascadero for the next five years, and all in all he enjoyed the experience. The

Above: Mary Ann Pesce was Anita Luchessa's roommate at university. The two girls were hitch-hiking when they met with Kemper.

LISTENING TO THE SEX OFFENDERS, KEMPER UNDERSTOOD THAT TO GET AWAY WITH RAPE IT WAS NECESSARY TO KILL THE VICTIM

Research Director, Dr Frank Vanasek, took him under his wing and Ed soon became a trusted inmate.

Gradually he acquired a basic working knowledge of psychological conditions, including his own. He knew what the doctors wanted him to say, and he said it.

But he also learned a lot about sex. Eagerly he listened to sex offenders of every kind, fantasizing at night about their experiences. He was particularly interested in the testimony of the rapists, noting that almost all of them had been caught because a victim had identified them. The moral seemed to be that to get away with rape, the victim should not be allowed to live.

These, of course, were very private thoughts. To the doctors, he tried to present the portrait of a rapidly improving, integrated human being.

Although the possibility of explosiveness was 'certainly evident', the doctors decided that he would be safe in the community. He was first released into the care of the California Youth Authority in 1969, and stayed there for three months while he attended college.

Most of his reports at Atascadero had noted that his mother was probably a causative influence of his problems, and recommended that Ed should in future be kept apart from her. But on his final release from the halfway house he was placed back in the custody of the formidable Clarnell Kemper just in time for his twenty-first birthday.

His mother had by now moved to the coastal town of Santa Cruz. She had an administrative job at the University of California and an apartment in the suburb of Aptos.

Across from the courtroom at Aptos was a bar named the Jury Room, where off-duty local policemen congregated. Kemper began drinking there, and his size, clipped hair, short, police-style moustache and conservative attitudes helped him fit in very well. The police liked him, and he became known to them as 'Big Eddie'.

Kemper, with his John Wayne fixation, fancied the idea of a career as a lawman himself, but was told that he would be too big for the California law agencies. He became depressed and took a job as

Above: *Fifteen-year-old Aiko Koo was standing at a bus stop in Berkeley, California when she was picked up by Ed Kemper.*

flagman with the Division of Highways.

His mother had other ideas. His marks had been good in college, during his treatment period, and she wanted him to enter university and 'better himself'. Inevitably they had rows.

The monotonous but steady job of flagman meant that Ed had independent money for the first time in his life. He bought a black and yellow 1969 Ford Galaxie sedan, and rented a room in a friend's flat in Alameda, a suburb of San Francisco.

PROWLING THE HIGHWAYS

For the next eighteen months or so, Ed Kemper spent his leisure time cruising the highways and byways of California, pondering in his unquiet mind lubriciously upon sex.

At the tail end of the 'flower power'

era, San Francisco and its environs were full of free-spirited young women who habitually hitch-hiked. Ed made a practice of picking them up and chatting to them, using all the psychological wiles he had learned in Atascadero.

His 'straight' looks led girls to trust him, and he made things easier for himself by getting his mother to fix him up with a University of California permit for his windscreen, giving him access to the university's campuses. He had given about 150 girls 'safe' lifts before he was ready for what he had in mind.

On Sunday, 7 May 1972, Kemper took to the access roads around the freeways outside San Francisco in his Ford Galaxie. Under his seat were a hunting knife, a plastic bag, a pair of handcuffs and a Browning 9mm automatic pistol, borrowed from a workmate. At 4 p.m. he spotted two pretty young girls thumbing by the side of the road, and Kemper drew alongside them.

Mary Ann Pesce and Anita Luchessa were eighteen years old, first-year students at Fresno State College. They were, as they told Kemper, going to see a friend at Stanford University, about an hour's drive away. The girls were unfamiliar with those parts, they admitted, and did not know the area.

As they talked, Kemper had been taking advantage of the girls' lack of local knowledge to drive out of town. Now he pulled down a side road. Mary Ann suddenly realized something was wrong and asked, from the back seat, 'What do you want?'

Kemper held up the Browning pistol in reply and said: 'You know what I want.'

Mary Ann talked calmly to Kemper in the approved fashion that she had learnt during university safety lectures, trying to get her potential attacker to see her as

*Above: **Ed Kemper helps police locate the body of his victim, Aiko Koo.***

*Below: **Police dig up the remains of fifteen-year-old Aiko Koo.***

a person rather than a victim. Unfortunately Kemper, with his experience at Atascadero, knew the ruse.

In fact he used a piece of psychology of his own. He told the girls that he was going to lock one of them in the boot and hide the other in the back seat, before taking them both back to his apartment. He had, of course, no such intention, but the girls went along with his wishes.

After locking the terrified Anita in the boot, he handcuffed Mary Ann's hands behind her back. Then he pulled a plastic bag over her head and began to strangle her with a dressing gown cord. Mary Ann put up a tremendous fight. She bit through the plastic bag and managed to get her mouth to the rope, keeping it from its choke-hold.

Kemper took up the hunting knife and stabbed her twice in the back. She turned over and he stabbed her once more, but she managed to shake the bag off and tried to sit upright. Finally Kemper grabbed her by the chin and slashed her throat.

With Mary Ann dead, Kemper went to deal with Anita, who must have heard the struggle and thus, he considered, would have to be slaughtered with despatch. He was right. When she saw the blood on his hands she began to scream and struggle and he stabbed frantically.

With both girls dead he drove the bodies back to his room in Alameda, knowing his flatmate was out. It was about 6 p.m. He carried them in, wrapped in blankets, and first undressed them, taking copious photographs with a Polaroid, and then dissected and decapitated them. He copied down the information from their ID cards and then destroyed their clothes and possessions, retaining only their ready cash – $8.28.

That same evening he took the segmented bodies out to the wilds of Santa Cruz, where he buried them. The heads he kept for a while. They were trophies, but they were also small guards against dental identification. Some time later he drove up into the hills and tumbled them into a ravine.

To the Californian police forces, the two girls were free spirits who had gone their own ways, regardless of parental admonitions. Mary Ann and Anita were, for a while, just a couple of runaways.

For four months Kemper gloated over his Polaroid photographs, slaking his sadistic urges by recalling in detail the things he had done to the two girls. Any intention to kill was further curbed by another motorcycle accident, which left him with a broken left arm.

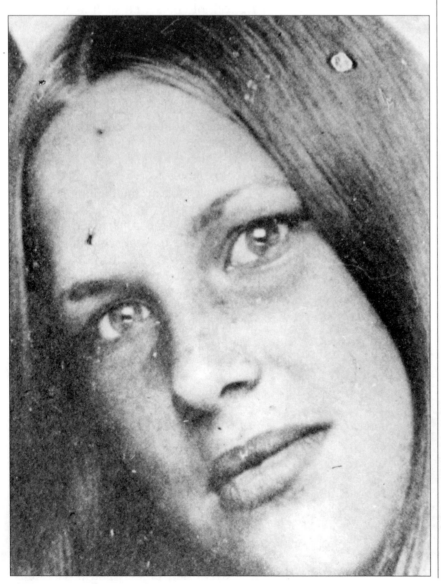

Below: *Eighteen-year-old Cindy Schall was picked up by Kemper on the outskirts of Santa Cruz.*

And Kemper had another priority on his mind. Any prospect of a better job was hampered by his record, for even in California few people fancied employing a double murderer who had served five years in a mental institution. Until he had his juvenile record declared sealed, he was unable to buy a gun easily. Meanwhile he had managed to borrow a .357 Magnum.

THE KILLER STRIKES AGAIN ... AND AGAIN

As dusk fell on 14 September, fifteen-year-old Aiko Koo was standing at a bus-stop in University Avenue, Berkeley, trying to thumb a lift.

Ed Kemper picked her up, but instead of taking her towards San Francisco, her destination, he set off fast down the coast highway. Aiko instantly realized she was in trouble and began to scream. Kemper pulled out his pistol and thrust it into her ribs, telling her that he meant her no harm. He was, he said, contemplating suicide, and wanted someone to talk to.

He drove her up into the mountains and stopped the car. Like her predecessors, Aiko struggled against his colossal weight, but in the end was overcome. He suffocated her into unconsciousness, raped her and then strangled her.

After wrapping the small body in a blanket and stowing it in the boot of his car Kemper drove off, glowing with satisfaction and the knowledge of his secret. A few miles down the road he stopped off at a bar for a beer, in order to savour his 'conquest' at leisure.

At about eleven that night he arrived back at Alameda and carried the body indoors. Then he dissected it and scattered the pieces in the Santa Cruz mountains. He retained only the head, which he carried around in the boot of his car.

On 15 September, a panel of juvenile psychiatrists examined Kemper and declared him mentally fit. Two months later a court, acting on the panel's instructions, 'sealed' his juvenile record. He was now entitled to go out to a gun shop, sign a form, wait five days and purchase a gun.

For the moment, however, Kemper had

VALID
WINTER 1973

niversity of California
Santa Cruz

STUDENT CARD

OID UNLESS VALIDATED ABOVE
FOR CURRENT TERM

THORPE ROSALIND H
MERRILL   09 49

557 84 1369   F

University of California
Santa Cruz

STUDENT CARD

VOID UNLESS VALIDATED BELOW
FOR CURRENT TERM

VALI
WINT
F/

LIU ALICE H
KRESGE   02 52

549 90 8420   F

Above: *Student IDs of Rosalind Thorpe and Alice Liu, the last two students to fall prey to Ed Kemper.*

other problems. His broken arm had kept him off work, and he was unable to pay the rent in Alameda. Reluctantly, he moved back to his mother's flat at 609A Ord Drive in Apatos. They began to quarrel again almost instantly, and the old frustrations began to build up.

On 8 January 1973, Kemper bought a .22 Rutgers automatic with a 6 inch barrel. Itching to try it out, he took to cruising the roads that same evening. Weather conditions seemed ideal, with heavy rain forcing girls who would otherwise avoid the risk to get any ride they could. He picked up two or three, but the streets were busy and he decided to make no untoward moves.

He had almost given up when, in

KEMPER USED HIS MOTHER'S WHITE SHOE POLISH TO COVER UP THE BLOODSTAINS ON HIS PLASTER CAST

Mission Avenue in Santa Cruz, he saw a short, shapely blonde named Cindy Schall.

Cindy was eighteen, a native of Marin County, near San Francisco. She was in her second year at Cabrillo College, on the outskirts of Santa Cruz, where she was studying to become a teacher. When Kemper picked her up she was on her way to an evening class.

As soon as she got into the car, he showed her the gun. Then he told her a similar 'suicide' story to the one he had told Aiko Koo. For three hours he drove, heading east to Watsonville and then turning into the hills at the township of Freedom. He persuaded her to get into the boot, and then killed her with a single shot to the head.

Kemper's mother was out for the evening, but even without the danger of prying eyes, Kemper had a difficult job manoeuvring the 11 stone corpse indoors with his injured arm. As it was, his plaster cast was splashed with blood, which he covered up with his mother's white shoe polish. Overnight, Cindy Schall lay in Kemper's bedroom cupboard.

The following morning, when his mother left for work, Kemper lugged the body into the bathroom and began cutting it into disposable pieces.

Later in the day, Kemper placed the pieces of flesh in plastic bags and threw them into a ravine near Monterey. As souvenirs he kept Cindy's outsize man's work shirt, and a small handmade ring. He also kept her head in his cupboard.

A day later, newspapers carried details of a Highway Patrolman's find on the road out of Monterey – two arms, a hand, and portions of two legs. Some time after that a ribcage was washed ashore. Enough of the body was recovered for Cindy Schall to be positively identified. Caution dictated that Ed get rid of the head, so he buried it outside his mother's window.

Just a month after the slaying of Cindy Schall, the Kempers – mother and son – had another mammoth row. The effect on Ed was familiar: rage and frustration. He stormed out of the house and threw himself into the Ford, tucking the pistol under his right thigh as he drove. It was another wet night.

Rosalind Thorpe was just emerging

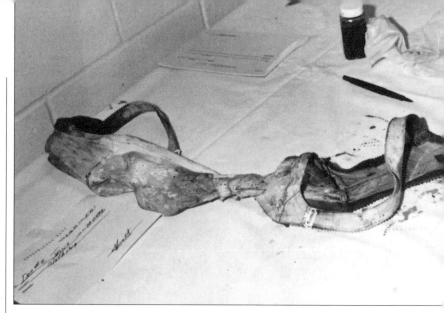

from a lecture theatre as Kemper drove by. Normally the twenty-three-year-old linguistics and psychology student rode her bicycle everywhere, but tonight the rain had put paid to that, she told Kemper. Seeing his campus sticker, she assumed him to be a fellow student.

As they chatted, Kemper spotted a small Chinese girl thumbing by the side of the road. He stopped and she got into the back seat. She was, she said, Alice Liu. She was twenty-one.

As they reached the hill overlooking the town of Santa Cruz, Kemper slowed the car as if to admire the lights reflected in the ocean. Then he picked up his gun in his good right hand and shot Rosalind smartly in the temple.

As she fell he turned to Alice, who was writhing in the back, screaming. Kemper fired twice at her and missed, then managed to hit her in the head. Alice lay unconscious, though making soft moaning sounds, as he drove at speed out of town.

For the first time in his 'adventures' Kemper felt sick and frightened at what he had done. Alice's moaning did not help, and as soon as he was far from any street lights he stopped the car and shot her once more in the head. For a time she was quiet, and then the terrible moaning began again. He pulled off the road and carried both bodies to the boot of his car.

His plaster cast was again sprayed with blood by the 'blow-back' as the bullet entered Rosalind's skull, and he stopped in a filling station toilet to scrub it off as best he could. Then he went home.

His mother was up, watching TV. He told her that he was going out for cigarettes, but before going to the shop he stopped by the car, opened the boot and hastily decapitated both bodies with his hunting knife. It was between 10 and 11p.m., but no one was around.

The following morning he carried Alice's headless body into his bedroom and had sexual intercourse with it, before cutting off her hands 'as an afterthought'. Later that day he dumped the bodies near San Francisco, in the hope that police would think the perpetrator a local man. Then he drove back to the town of Pacifica and threw the heads and hands over a bluff called Devil's Slide.

Above: *Rosalind Thorpe's bloodstained bra was introduced as evidence at Kemper's trial.*

TROUBLE NOW CAME FROM AN UNEXPECTED QUARTER - ANOTHER MASS MURDERER WAS WORKING OUT OF SANTA CRUZ

HIS MOTHER ASKED HER SON IF HE WANTED TO TALK. 'NO,' HE REPLIED, AND WENT TO FETCH A KNIFE AND HAMMER

He also felt that things were getting more difficult for him. At the end of January a woman's skeleton was found in the mountains. She was identified as Mary Guilfoyle, a twenty-three-year-old English student who, like Cindy Schall, had attended Cabrillo College.

She was a victim not of Kemper but of another mass murderer, Herbert Mullin, who had started killing at the same time as Kemper and also lived in Santa Cruz. Mullin was to kill thirteen victims and eventually ended up in the same prison as Ed Kemper. Meanwhile he was causing Kemper trouble.

FINAL BLOODBATH

In the middle of April, Kemper packed up all the documents and personal belongings he had taken from his victims, together with his prized .22 pistol, and threw them in the ocean. He had stomach trouble, which turned out to be ulcers, and his nerves were in shreds. It was time, he felt, to bring his career to a massive climax, perhaps killing everyone in his neighbourhood in one night of slaughter.

On 20 April, Good Friday, Kemper went home and drank beer in front of the television while pondering what to do next; his mother was working late. At about four in the morning of Easter Saturday he went into his mother's bedroom. She was awake, and asked him if he wanted to talk. He told him no, and went back to his own room to fetch a pocket knife and a hammer.

When he was sure his mother was sleeping he crept back in and brought the hammer down with all his force on the right side of her head. She did not move, but as the blood welled up Ed saw that she was still breathing. Turning her over on to her back, he sawed into her trachea with his pocket knife, continuing to cut until the head rolled free.

For the rest of that day he felt sick, giddy and restless. The killing this time had done nothing to calm his confused feelings. He cleaned up the bloody mess as best he could, and then went out drinking with a friend.

Towards the evening, in a muddled attempt to disguise his mother's absence over the Easter holiday, he decided to kill her best friend, Mrs Sally Hallett. He hoped that the joint disappearance would confuse the police. Kemper rang Mrs Hallett, and told her he was preparing a surprise dinner for his mother. Mrs Hallett agreed to come over that evening.

She arrived exhausted after the journey. 'Let's sit down,' she said. 'I'm dead!' They were her last words.

After strangling and decapitating her, Kemper went for a drink at the Jury Room. He had, he knew, reached the very end of the trail. There was no way he could cover up the slaughter just across the road from the policemen's bar.

On Easter Sunday morning he packed Mrs Hallett's body into his bedroom cupboard, and then loaded his weapons into her car.

He headed east to Reno and then hired a car, leaving Mrs Hallett's vehicle at a garage. He drove for the rest of the day and night. Just before midnight on Monday, 23 April, he stopped at a pay-phone in the town of Pueblo, Colorado, 1200 miles away from Santa Cruz.

Then he rang the Santa Cruz police and asked for Lieutenant Charles Scherer, who was in charge of the student murder investigations. It was not until three telephone calls and five more hours had passed, however, that Ed Kemper convinced his old police drinking buddies that he was the man they were looking for. They sent a Colorado patrol car out to pick him up, and he was arrested in Denver by Santa Cruz police.

Ed Kemper's confession was long, articulate and complete in every detail, for he had savoured each killing over and over in his head. When the details of his release from Atascadero were made public there was sudden public loss of confidence in psychiatric criminal evaluation. It was already shaky after revelations that Herbert Mullin, the other Santa Cruz murderer, who had also been arrested, was likewise a former mental hospital inmate. Typically Ed Kemper detested Mullin because 'he had killed people for no good reason'.

On 25 October 1973 Ed Kemper was charged with eight counts of first degree murder at Santa Cruz Court House. On 8 November he was found guilty and sentenced to life imprisonment in California Medical Facility at Vacaville. He escaped the death penalty because it was suspended in California at that time.

All parole recommendations for Kemper have been turned down since then, and it is unlikely that he will ever be released. Since entering the Facility, Kemper has worked at recording books for the blind, supervising fifteen fellow inmates. He received a public service award for this work in 1981.

'LET'S SIT DOWN,' SAID HIS MOTHER'S FRIEND AFTER HER EXHAUSTING JOURNEY. 'I'M DEAD!' A FEW MINUTES LATER, SHE WAS

Below: *Ed Kemper towers above his police escort in court.*

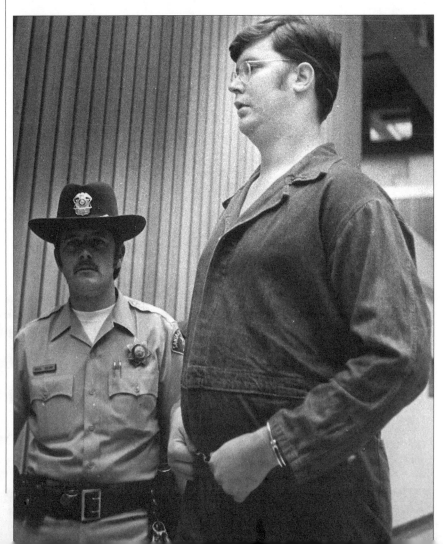

DENNIS NILSEN
A Quiet Civil Servant

Was it fear of desertion that caused Dennis Nilsen to become a mass murderer in the most gruesome of circumstances? And was he merely evil, or was he himself one of life's victims – a schizophrenic?

At 6.25 on the morning of 8 February 1983, Michael Cattran parked his Dyno-Rod van outside 23 Cranley Gardens in the north London suburb of Muswell Hill. It was a routine call. Jim Allcock, one of the residents of No. 23, had phoned to say that the drains had

Above: *A police constable stands guard at the back of 23 Cranley Gardens, Muswell Hill, where Dennis Nilsen rented an attic flat.*

Opposite: *Dennis Nilsen, the quiet civil servant who became Britain's most prolific mass murderer.*

AT THE BOTTOM OF THE STINKING SHAFT WAS A GLUTINOUS, GREYISH-WHITE SUBSTANCE

Left: *The front of 23 Cranley Gardens.*

been blocked for five days. After a quick examination of the interior plumbing, Cattran decided the problem lay outside the house itself. He walked round to the side of the house and removed the manhole cover.

The smell was nauseating as Cattran climbed down the 12-foot inspection shaft. At the bottom he found a glutinous greyish-white mass.

Cattran told Jim Allcock that it was nothing serious and that he would be back shortly to straighten things out. When he called his boss, however, he voiced his real suspicions. The matter which was clogging the drains at 23 Cranley Gardens was, in his opinion, human flesh.

Cattran and his boss returned to Muswell Hill the following morning. To Cattran's surprise, the glutinous mass had vanished. He knew that, even though it had been raining the previous day, the drains could not possibly have cleared themselves. Cattran reached deep into the drainpipe and pulled out several pieces of meat and a number of bones.

Cattran explained the mystery of the missing sludge to Jim Allcock and another tenant, Fiona Bridges. They told

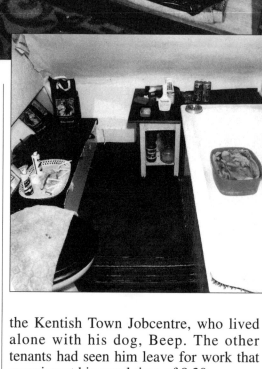

him they had heard someone moving the manhole cover in the early hours of the morning. They thought it might be Mr Nilsen who lived above them in the attic flat. Cattran and his boss decided it was time to call the police.

Detective Chief Inspector Peter Jay arrived on the scene shortly after 11a.m. and collected the meat and bones for forensic examination. At Charing Cross Hospital, it took pathologist Professor David Bowen only minutes to confirm that the meat was indeed human flesh and that the bones were from a man's hand.

THE TENANT OF THE ATTIC FLAT

Police attention immediately focused on the occupier of the attic flat, Dennis Andrew Nilsen, an executive officer at

Above left: *The stove in Nilsen's kitchen was caked with grease. Forensic examination determined that this was human fat.*

Above: *Black plastic bags in Nilsen's wardrobe contained the remains of two bodies.*

Right: *Two bodies had been dissected in Nilsen's bath, and the remains of Stephen Sinclair had been hidden under it.*

Below: *A cooking pot used by Nilsen to simmer the head of one of his victims.*

the Kentish Town Jobcentre, who lived alone with his dog, Beep. The other tenants had seen him leave for work that morning at his usual time of 8.30.

Peter Jay, together with Detective Inspector McCusker and Detective Constable Butler, waited outside 23 Cranley Gardens for Nilsen to return.

When he walked up to the front door at 5.40, Peter Jay intercepted him. Nilsen, a polite, quietly spoken man in his late thirties, seemed surprised but not alarmed when Jay introduced himself and his colleagues as police officers.

The four men went inside the house and climbed the stairs to Nilsen's tiny flat. Once inside, Jay told Nilsen about the human flesh which had been found in the drain outside. Nilsen feigned horror, but Jay was not remotely convinced. 'Stop messing about,' he said. 'Where's the rest of the body?'

Nilsen didn't even bother to protest his innocence. 'In two plastic bags in the wardrobe. I'll show you,' he said, unlocking the doors. The awful stench from the cupboard confirmed that Nilsen was telling the truth.

He arrested Nilsen, charged him with murder and shipped him off to Hornsey Police Station.

En route, Inspector McCusker asked Nilsen if there was anything he wanted to say. Nilsen replied, 'It's a long story. It goes back a long time. I'll tell you everything. I want to get it off my chest.'

'Are we talking about one body or two?' McCusker asked Nilsen.

'Fifteen or sixteen,' Nilsen replied calmly. 'Since 1978.... Three at Cranley Gardens and about thirteen at my previous address, 195 Melrose Avenue in Cricklewood.'

CONTENTS OF A WARDROBE

Detective Chief Inspector Jay returned to 23 Cranley Gardens with Detective Chief Superintendent Chambers and the pathologist, Professor Bowen. They removed the two stinking black plastic bags from Nilsen's wardrobe and took them to Hornsey mortuary.

When Bowen opened the first he found it contained four smaller shopping bags. In the first of these was the left-hand side of a man's chest with the arm attached. The second contained the right-hand side of a chest. The third held a torso, and the fourth an assortment of human offal.

In the other black bag, Bowen found two human heads and another torso with the arms attached but missing the hands. One of the heads had most of the flesh boiled away.

Nilsen told the police that one of the heads belonged to a young drug addict called Stephen Sinclair. The second he knew only as 'John the Guardsman'. He could put no name to a third victim whose remains were later found in a tea chest at his flat.

Nilsen seemed willing, even anxious, to help the police. On 11 February, three days after his arrest, he accompanied Peter Jay to the ground-floor flat at 195 Melrose Avenue which he had occupied from 1976 to 1981.

'ARE WE TALKING ABOUT ONE BODY OR TWO?' ENQUIRED THE POLICEMAN. 'FIFTEEN OR SIXTEEN,' WAS THE CALM REPLY

Below: *Nilsen's obsession with death was already evident during his days in the National Service.*

He told Jay that he had cut up the bodies and burnt them on a series of huge bonfires in the back garden. He even pointed out where the fires had been and where they should look for human remains.

Using this information, forensic teams started the laborious task of sifting through the earth for evidence. A day later they had found enough human ash and bone fragments to establish that at least eight people had been cremated in the garden.

Despite his willingness to cooperate with the police, Nilsen was unable to identify many of his early victims. None of them had ever been more than casual acquaintances. They had been, for the most part, young, homeless homosexuals – social misfits, drug addicts or alcoholics, men who could simply disappear without anyone knowing or caring. However, based on dates and

physical descriptions given by Nilsen, and comparing them with missing persons' records, the police were eventually able to identify six victims with reasonable certainty.

The question now for the police and Nilsen's lawyer was not if Nilsen was a mass murderer, but rather why he had killed more than a dozen young men. On this point, Nilsen could not help. 'I am hoping you will tell me that,' he said.

FOUR YEARS OF CARNAGE

Nilsen was questioned for the next few weeks, during which time he gave a meticulous account of his four years of carnage. It was a story so monstrous and grotesque that it made even case-hardened police interrogators physically ill to listen to it.

It had all started on New Year's Eve 1978. Nilsen had met a young Irish boy in a pub in the West End and taken him back to his flat in Melrose Avenue. After seeing in the New Year, the two men had gone to bed together. They were both stupefied with drink, and no sex took place between them.

In the morning, according to Nilsen, he woke to find the young Irishman still asleep beside him. He was suddenly overcome with terror that the boy would want to leave as soon as he too awoke. Nilsen desperately wanted him to stay, and could only think of one way to ensure that he did so.

Nilsen picked up a tie from the floor, straddled the boy's chest, placed the tie around his neck and pulled. The boy woke and a mighty struggle ensued before he finally passed out.

But he was not dead yet. So Nilsen went to the kitchen, filled a bucket with water and held the boy's head under the water until he drowned.

Nilsen then bathed the boy's body, dressed it in clean underwear and socks, took it back to bed with him and masturbated. For the next week, Nilsen went off to work as usual. He returned each evening to his dead companion who would be sitting in an armchair, waiting for him.

After eight days, Nilsen prised up some floor boards and hid the corpse. It

Above: After a brief stint with the police, Nilsen, aged 28, spent three months working as a security guard.

Below: In the winter of 1975, Nilsen moved into a ground floor flat at 195 Melrose Avenue. It was here that he committed a dozen murders.

remained there for seven months before Nilsen dissected it and burnt it on a bonfire in his back garden.

On the evening of 3 December 1979, almost a year later, Dennis Nilsen was cruising the gay bars of Soho when he met a twenty-six-year-old Canadian tourist, Kenneth Ockendon. Ockendon, who was staying at a cheap hotel in King's Cross, was due to fly home the following day.

Nilsen persuaded him to accompany him back to Melrose Avenue for a meal. He could stay the night if he wanted, and pick up his things from the hotel the following morning.

By the early hours of the morning the two men were in Nilsen's sitting room, both much the worse for drink. Nilsen was watching Ockendon as he listened to music through a set of headphones.

His feelings of imminent desertion were similar to those he had experienced a year earlier.

So Nilsen walked behind Ockendon's chair, grabbed the flex of the headphones and strangled him with it. Again he

built an enormous bonfire which was constructed in part from human remains wrapped in carpet. He crowned the fire with an old car tyre to disguise the smell of burning flesh.

At the end of 1981, Nilsen was planning to move. By this time he had accumulated a further five bodies and, shortly before he left, he had another massive fire.

No. 23 Cranley Gardens, Nilsen's new home, presented some real problems for a mass murderer of his ilk. It was an attic flat with no floorboards and no garden – in fact nowhere decent to hide a body at all. But this didn't stop him.

Within weeks of his move to Muswell Hill, Nilsen strangled John Howlett with an upholstery strap and then drowned him. Graham Allen was the next to die. Nilsen couldn't actually recall killing him, but thought he had strangled him with a tie while he was eating an omelette.

On 26 January Nilsen met his last victim. Stephen Sinclair, a drug addict and petty criminal, was wandering the streets of Soho looking for a hand-out. Nilsen offered to buy him a hamburger and then persuaded him to go back to Cranley Gardens with him.

Two weeks later, Michael Cattran of Dyno-Rod found what was left of Stephen in the drain outside 23 Cranley Gardens.

NO EMOTION, NO REMORSE

On 24 October 1983, Dennis Andrew Nilsen stood before Mr Justice Croom-Johnson at No. 1 Court in the Old Bailey. He was charged with six murders and two attempted murders.

There was no doubt that Nilsen had committed the offences. What the court had to evaluate was Nilsen's mental state at the time when he committed them.

If Nilsen had pleaded Guilty, as he originally intended, he would have saved the jury a considerable ordeal. Instead, they were forced to spend two weeks listening to detailed evidence of Nilsen's gruesome acts.

Detective Chief Superintendent Chambers spent almost an entire day reading out a transcript of Nilsen's

washed the body, dressed it in clean underwear, placed it next to him in bed and went to sleep.

Ockendon's corpse remained his constant companion for the next two weeks. Nilsen spent the evenings watching television with the body in an armchair next to him. When he was ready for bed, he would wrap it in a curtain and place it under the floorboards for the night.

Unlike the Irish boy, Ockendon's disappearance caused a considerable stir. Several of the tabloids carried his picture and Nilsen felt sure that his days were numbered. But the police didn't come. And over the next eighteen months eleven more young men were destined to die at Melrose Avenue.

By the end of 1980, Nilsen had accumulated six bodies. Three were stowed under the floorboards, while the others were cut up, stuffed in suitcases and stored in a garden shed.

At the beginning of December, Nilsen

Above: *Police remove human remains from Nilsen's flat at Melrose Avenue.*

EVERY EVENING NILSEN WOULD WATCH TELEVISION WITH OCKENDON'S BODY IN AN ARMCHAIR NEXT TO HIM

WITH NO FLOORBOARDS AND NO GARDEN, HOW WAS NILSEN GOING TO DISPOSE OF HIS VICTIMS AT HIS NEW ADDRESS?

confession. The graphic descriptions of decapitations and dissections, of the boiling and mincing of human flesh, and of necrophilia, sickened and enraged the jury. Nilsen, for his part, sat through the evidence without betraying a single vestige of emotion.

The prosecution called three witnesses to give evidence that Nilsen had attempted to kill them. Paul Nobbs, a university student, told how he had been rescued by Nilsen from the unwanted attentions of another man.

Nilsen had taken him back to Cranley Gardens and had shown him genuine kindness. He had not tried to ply him with drink or force him to have sex. He had even suggested that he call his mother so that she would not be worried. Nobbs had gone to bed alone but had woken in the early hours of the morning with a splitting headache. He had looked in the mirror and had seen that his eyes were completely bloodshot and that there was a bruise around his neck.

Nilsen had feigned concern, saying that Nobbs looked awful and should go straight to a doctor.

At the casualty department of the hospital he went to, Nobbs was told that he had been partially strangled. He had realized that Nilsen must have been his attacker, but had been reluctant to report the incident to the police because he felt sure that he would not be believed.

The defence made much of Nobbs's testimony. It demonstrated that Nilsen could behave perfectly normally one minute and then be possessed of murderous impulses the next, without provocation or reason. It proved, they said, that Nilsen was clearly insane.

If Nobbs's story was difficult to credit, Karl Strotter's encounter with Nilsen was nothing short of fantastic. Strotter had met Nilsen in a pub in Camden Town. He was depressed after the break-up of a relationship and, like Nobbs, he described Nilsen's behaviour towards him as sympathetic and undemanding.

They had gone back to Cranley Gardens together and Nilsen had put him to bed in a sleeping bag. Strotter described what happened next: 'I woke up feeling something round my neck. My head was hurting and I couldn't breathe

Above: *Having confessed his crimes, Nilsen is remanded at Highgate Magistrates' Court in north London.*

NOBBS WOKE UP WITH BLOODSHOT EYES AND A SPLITTING HEADACHE. DOCTORS TOLD HIM SOMEONE HAD TRIED TO STRANGLE HIM

properly and I wondered what it was.

'I felt his hand pulling at the zip at the back of my neck. He was saying in a sort of whispered shouting voice, "Stay still. Stay still." I thought perhaps he was trying to help me out of the sleeping bag because I thought I had got caught up in the zip, which he had warned me about. Then I passed out.

'...the pressure was increasing. My head was hurting and I couldn't breathe. I remember vaguely hearing water running. I remember vaguely being carried and then felt very cold. I knew I was in the water and he was trying to drown me. He kept pushing me into the water....I just thought I was dying. I thought: "You are drowning. This is what it feels like to die." I felt very relaxed and I passed out. I couldn't fight any more.'

Strotter said he was amazed to awake lying on a sofa with Nilsen massaging him. Nilsen had then helped him to the underground station and wished him luck.

This apparent detachment from reality was echoed in Detective Chief Inspector Jay's evidence as he described Nilsen's behaviour during his interrogation. He was, Jay said, relaxed, cooperative and matter-of-fact. He did not, however, show any remorse. It was as though he was talking about someone else.

Both the prosecution and defence trotted out their 'expert witnesses', a mandatory feature of insanity pleas. Two equally well-qualified psychiatrists proceeded to give directly conflicting evaluations of the mental condition of the accused, thus effectively cancelling one another out in the eyes of the jury.

The judge spent four hours summing up, addressing himself in particular to the question of Nilsen's personality. 'A mind can be evil without being abnormal,' he advised the jury. 'There must be no excuses for Nilsen if he has moral defects. A nasty nature is not arrested or retarded development of the mind.'

The implication of what Mr Croom-Johnson was saying was obvious. Dennis Nilsen was, in his opinion, evil rather than insane, and the jury should therefore find him guilty of murder.

The jury retired on the morning of Thursday, 3 November 1983. Despite the clear guidance given by the judge, they returned the following morning to say that they were unable to reach a

Above: *Two that got away: Douglas Stewart (left)*; *Karl Stotter (right). Both testified at the trial that they had been victims of attacks by Dennis Nilsen. Their evidence was vital for the prosecution as it argued that Nilsen was not technically insane.*

Below: *Nilsen's face bears the scar from an attack by a fellow prisoner.*

consensus about Nilsen's state of mind at the time of the various murders.

Mr Croom-Johnson said that he would accept a majority verdict. At 4.25 that afternoon the jury returned to court with a verdict of Guilty on all six counts of murder, by a majority of ten to two.

The judge condemned Dennis Andrew Nilsen to life imprisonment, with the recommendation that he should serve no less than twenty-five years.

Nilsen spent the first nine months of his sentence in Parkhurst Prison on the Isle of Wight.

In the summer of 1984 Nilsen was transferred to Wakefield Prison. He remains there to this day, sharing his cell with a budgerigar called Hamish.

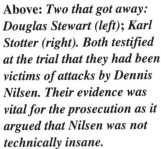

DR PERERA
The Arrogant Dentist

A smooth and well-educated murderer thought he could outwit a simple Yorkshire detective. But he had not bargained for police perseverance and expert assistance in putting together the gruesome evidence that eventually convicted him

In 1935 Bukhtyar Hakim, a Parsee doctor who had changed his name to Buck Ruxton when he settled in the northern English town of Lancaster, strangled his wife Isabella in a fit of jealous rage. The sound of the struggle brought her maid, Mary Rogerson, to the scene. Ruxton killed her too.

He took the bodies upstairs and cut them into small pieces in the bath before wrapping them in newspapers and strips of cotton sheet. Then he drove north and scattered the packages along the side of the Edinburgh–Moffat road.

Ruxton was eventually arrested and brought to the gallows at Lancaster Gaol.

At some time during the early winter of 1983 history, in the person of Dr

Above: *DI Tom Hodgson, who spent a year gradually building up a case against Dr Perera.*

Opposite: *Dr Perera is taken away by the police.*

Below: *Perera's house in Sitwell Close, in the Wakefield suburb of Sandal.*

Samuel Perera, repeated itself almost detail for detail when Perera killed and cut to pieces his adopted daughter.

Like Ruxton, Perera was a native of the Indian subcontinent, having been born in Sri Lanka, at that time the British colony of Ceylon. He too was a doctor, a specialist in oral biology at Leeds University School of Medicine. He lived near Wakefield, West Yorkshire, just fifty miles from Lancaster. And, like Ruxton, he was astonishingly arrogant.

As one detective who worked on the case was to put it: 'He must have known of Ruxton from his medical studies. All doctors do a course in forensic medicine, and Ruxton is a standard text. You'd have thought that he would have learned from Ruxton's mistakes.'

Perera was born in 1943. After graduating from Colombo University he travelled to England to take up a three-year research scholarship at Newcastle University dental school. There he met and married his Hindu wife Dammika, converting her to Roman Catholicism.

In the early seventies he successfully applied for a post as lecturer in oral biology in the Dental Department of the Leeds School of Medicine, and travelled to England to settle in the middle-class suburb of Sandal, near Wakefield.

Above: *Nilanthe 'Philomena Perera', the Sri Lankan girl adopted by Dr Perera.*

JUNGLE GIRL

Mrs Perera gave birth to two daughters during the latter part of the 1970s. But in December 1981, for reasons which were never satisfactorily explained, her husband decided he wanted to adopt a further child. He and his wife went back to Sri Lanka and returned with a ten-year-old girl named Nilanthe, giving her the adoptive name of Philomena. Perera may have had long-term plans to use Philomena as a sort of household slave. He had paid money to her natural father and, as he was later to tell police dismissively, 'in any case she was only a jungle girl'.

Over the next couple of years the little 'jungle girl' became known and liked by the other residents of Sitwell Close. Her lack of English gave her a somewhat forlorn attitude, but her waif-like figure, large doe eyes and long, glossy hair held the promise of great beauty.

In November 1983, Nilanthe 'Philomena' Perera disappeared. 'My husband is very strict,' Mrs Perera told a neighbour. 'He has banned her from going out because she would make eyes at the men.'

But Christmas came and went, winter gave way to spring and there was still no sign of little Philomena.

The neighbours' curiosity began to stir again and finally, in April 1984, Mrs Perera told them: 'She's gone home. She grew very homesick and my husband decided it was kindest to send her back to her father in Sri Lanka.'

LETTER TO THE LAW

But the neighbours were not satisfied, and so they did a rather un-English thing. They called a meeting and, after discussing the matter, decided to send a letter laying out the facts to the authorities. The letter was opened at Wood Street Police Station in Wakefield, by a fifty-one-year-old detective inspector named Tom Hodgson.

Hodgson was a burly, snub-nosed man with a stubborn, cleft chin. His receding hairline and the bags under his amiable eyes bespoke years of police service, mostly as a detective officer.

It was a warm summer morning in July 1984 when Detective Inspector Hodgson drove up to 16 Sitwell Close, at the beginning of what was to be a year-long investigation – and Hodgson's last case.

From that first meeting, the detective later claimed, he was struck by the smooth doctor's exaggerated sense of his own importance. As he ushered his visitor through the front door, Perera snapped at his wife: 'Get upstairs with the children.'

'She's only a wife, after all,' he told Hodgson. Seated in Perera's front room, the policeman told him that he was

Above: *Philomena's home in Sri Lanka.*

Left: *Philomena's mother.*

making routine enquiries about the missing girl Nilanthe Philomena. Dr Perera was easy in his reply. Philomena, he said, had failed to settle, growing more and more homesick as the months passed. 'After all she was only a jungle girl.'

In April, he said, he had decided to take her home. He had taken her with him on a weekend trip to Catania in Sicily, where his brother lived. From

---

FROM THEIR FIRST MEETING DETECTIVE INSPECTOR HODGSON WAS STRUCK BY PERERA'S ARROGANT SELF-ASSURANCE

---

there, the brother was to have put her on a flight to Sri Lanka.

Tom Hodgson returned to his desk at Wood Street to set in motion a long and careful series of checks, first with the airport authorities and then with Interpol.

First, the airport authorities: had Dr Perera booked a flight to Sicily with his adopted daughter from any British airport at any time in the early months of the year? No.

Next, Interpol came back to Hodgson with the result of their enquiries in Sicily and Sri Lanka. The girl had not turned up there. It seemed likely, therefore, that she must still be in the British Isles.

Meanwhile, Hodgson had paid several surreptitious visits to the Dental Department of Leeds Medical School, winkling out details of Dr Perera and his ways. 'Arrogant' was the word repeatedly used by his colleagues of Perera.

SEARCH FOR THE BODY

By now, Hodgson had no doubt in his own mind that Perera was a murderer. But where was the body? Hodgson's best course of action seemed to lie in shaking Perera into making some kind of a move – perhaps shifting the body to a safer hiding-place. To this end the tenacious

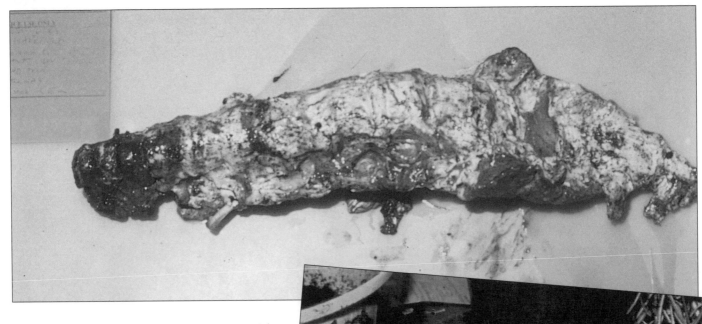

Yorkshireman began to play a cat and mouse game with the doctor, making it clear to him that he was being watched – 'showing out', in police parlance – and making several personal calls at his home to interview him on small points.

Just before Christmas 1984, Inspector Hodgson decided to give his quarry a good shake-up. 'I knew by this time that something was seriously wrong, so I started to put pressure on him. I told him I was coming to see him at the university on the first day of the new term in January 1985. Perera started blustering, saying I was making assertions I could not prove.'

And then, on 4 February 1985, came dramatic evidence to justify Hodgson's pressure tactics. A colleague of Perera's who shared a desk and cupboards with him noticed a large brown envelope in one of the desk drawers. It contained a human jawbone with several teeth present, and a number of pieces of human skull. Aware of the police interest in Dr Perera, the lecturer made a rapid search of other drawers and cupboards used by the Sri Lankan. He found a five-litre glass beaker, a coffee jar with a screw-top lid, and a shallow, stainless steel tray. Each of these contained small bones and bone fragments, immersed in a bluish liquid which later proved to be a decalcifying fluid which would ultimately have dissolved the bones completely. None of these bones appeared to have anything to do with orthodox dental research.

Top: *A piece of human spine found in a plant pot in Perera's house.*

Above: *Pieces of human flesh were found under geranium plants in two other pots.*

A UNIVERSITY COLLEAGUE NOTICED AMONG PERERA'S BELONGINGS A BROWN ENVELOPE CONTAINING HUMAN BONES

The lecturer telephoned Wood Street Police Station, and Hodgson arranged for the remains to be transferred to Wakefield. He also arranged for Dr Perera to come to the station to assist the police with their enquiries.

Early the next morning, Mrs Perera and her two children were taken into care from the house in Sitwell Close. Overall-clad policemen arrived at their home with spades, trowels and gardener's riddles.

THE SEARCH FOR EVIDENCE

The police eventually turned to the Department of Forensic Medicine at Sheffield University. Head of the department and holder of the chair of forensic pathology at the university was Professor Alan Usher, whose active career spanned over thirty years.

Several identical 'murder bags' containing equipment for on-site investigation were always kept packed and ready in Professor Usher's office. On receiving Hodgson's call he picked one up, loaded it into his car, and set off on the hour-long drive to Wakefield and the suburb of Sandal.

When he arrived, the police were already digging in the garden at Sitwell Close. Between the rear of the garage and the garden fence they had excavated an oblong hole about five feet by three feet, and were sieving the earth through large garden riddles. On a plastic sheet by the hole lay a tooth, a small bone and a long hank of dark, earth-clotted hair.

A brief examination convinced Usher that the bone and tooth were human. They were docketed and placed in samples envelopes for later scrutiny.

As the police continued their digging outside, Usher and the two senior detectives entered the hallway of the house. The first objects to confront them were three large plastic plant pots. The central one was raised, and contained a narrow leaved plant. The other two, containing geraniums, stood on the floor on either side.

'The plants seemed very small for such large pots,' recalled Professor Usher, 'and they didn't seem to be doing terribly well. They were wilting somewhat.' When the professor bent to examine them further he caught a distinct whiff of the sickly-sweet stench of decaying flesh.

Ouside the door stood a plastic dustbin. Usher placed its upturned lid on the ground and very carefully decanted the contents of the central plant pot on to this ad hoc examination table.

What met their eyes gave Chief Superintendent Walter Cowman, at least, one of the more unpleasant frissons of his long career. 'I don't think I shall ever forget,' he said later, 'the sight of a virtually complete human spine curled around the roots of the plant.'

The two geranium pots were emptied in turn. Plant, earth and roots slid out in a solid lump, revealing that the geraniums

were embedded in some browning, slimy material. It was rotting human flesh.

Eventually Professor Usher's team were to identify a total of 106 bony fragments which, in their opinion, came from 77 individual bones or parts of bones. They had been gathered from eight different sites – four at home, four in the Leeds lab – accessible to Samuel Perera.

PIECING TOGETHER A HUMAN JIGSAW

But that was in the future. In that second week of February 1985, Usher was faced with the long and tedious task of 'defatting' the bones. This meant stripping them of their remaining fat and flesh, and then with infinite care attaching numbers to them so that each tiny piece of the jigsaw could be identified, and the source not be lost, as attempts were made to rearticulate them into the semblance of a skeleton.

It was a colossal project, and one of the most complex ever undertaken. Over a period of time Usher assembled a

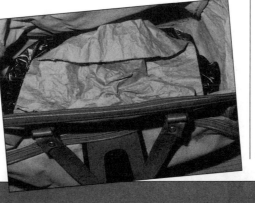

Left and below: *A holdall was found containing a collection of human bones.*

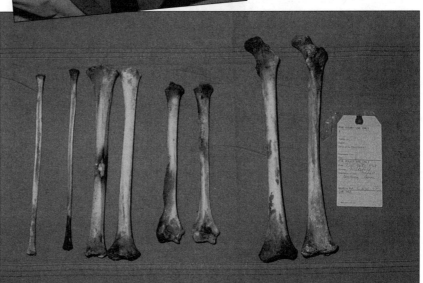

seven-man team of distinguished experts, headed by himself.

The anatomist's role was filled by Professor G.N.C. Crawford. Then there were Professor R.D. Grainger, Professor of Radiodiagnosis at Sheffield Medical School; Dr G.T. Craig, senior lecturer in oral pathology at Sheffield University and an expert in forensic dentistry; Dr Y.Z. Erzinclioglu, an entomologist from Cambridge University – brought in to study organisms in the soil; Dr P.J. Tarff, a postgraduate student, and Mr D.R. Jarvis, Usher's senior medical scientific officer.

SCIENTIFIC KNOW-HOW

The deliberations of the seven experts took several months, for they had several vital points to establish: points which should eventually satisfy a court of law.

First, were the bones human, and were they the bones of one person only? The answers to both questions were affirmative. Second, what of sex? In general the bones were gracile and slender, with little evidence of any strong muscular markings: 'Though not conclusive in themselves, the delicacy of the bones and the lack of muscular development are predominantly female characteristics,' said Professor Usher, 'and these facts, coupled with the pelvic angles and Professor Grainger's radiological studies, satisfied us that these were the bones of a female.'

Like sex, the determination of age was difficult from the incomplete remains. In the end, Usher took data from previous

Above: *A tray of bone fragments in decalcifying fluid was found in the laboratory where Perera worked.*

Below: *Police digging up Perera's garden in the search for evidence.*

enquiries in conjunction with independent assessments made by Professor Grainger, radiologically, and Dr Craig, using dental methods, and came to the firm conclusion that the remains were those of a person 'certainly not seventeen years old and most probably between twelve and fifteen years old at the time of death'.

The establishment of the exact race of the dead person proved, in the end, impossible. Again the bones were so fragmented that little significance could be made of, for instance, skull shape. However, Dr Craig found certain deposits on the front upper and lower molar to be so unusual as to suggest that the skeleton was not Caucasian.

As this complicated work was being carried out at the Sheffield Medico-Legal Centre, a team from the University's Department of Television and Graphics was preparing a series of charts showing the bones recovered in relation to the average human skeleton. These charts would later prove invaluable in court.

For it was towards the criminal courts, of course, that these enquiries were inexorably heading.

The entomological studies performed by Dr Erzinclioglu were in themselves proving quite damning to Dr Perera. Tiny insect pupae on many of the bones showed that they had first been buried at an outdoor site – and soil samples matched those of the Sitwell Close garden – before being transferred indoors, first beneath the house floor and then into the oral biology laboratories at Leeds University.

The degree of putrefaction found in the

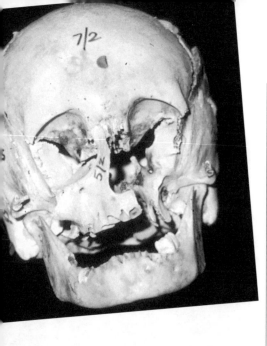

Left: *The reconstructed skull of the victim.*

THE SUSPECT CLAIMED THAT THE FLESH IN THE FLOWER POTS WAS PORK, WHICH HE WAS EXPERIMENTING WITH AS A FERTILIZER

---

mass of flesh in the central plant pot meant that death had occurred at least six months prior to discovery and possibly a great deal earlier than that. 'What it all came down to,' remarked Professor Usher dryly, 'was that I could conceive of no legitimate purpose for what was literally half a human torso being concealed in a domestic flower pot.'

By now Perera was, as one detective put it, 'losing some of his cool'. First, he claimed that the flesh in the flower pots had been pork, which he was trying as a new kind of fertilizer. Analysis of the flesh proved this to be palpable nonsense.

Then he claimed that the partial destruction of bones in his laboratory was necessary to his research work. While it is true that decalcification of bone does play a part in dental pathology, the samples used are invariably small – usually no bigger than a postage stamp. And the study of ribs, pelvises and long bones is hardly relevant to dental medicine.

'It simply wasn't possible, due to the fragmentary nature of the remains, to come to any firm conclusion as to the cause of the young girl's death,' admitted Professor Usher.

'But from the systematic attempts made to destroy and dispose of her body, I would strongly deduce that she died of foul play. All indications were that this was the body of Nilanthe Philomena Perera.'

In desperation, Perera tried one last ploy. His new story was that he had

Below: *Professor Usher sifting through the contents of the plant pots.*

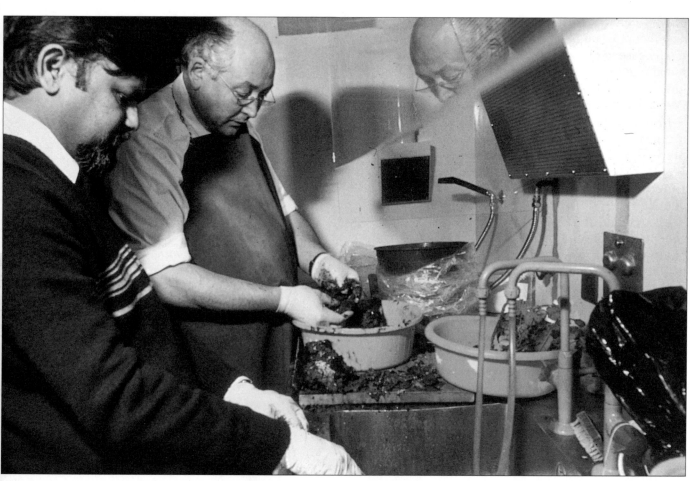

obtained the corpse of a young girl legitimately from a Sri Lankan university for medical purposes and had brought it to England in his suitcase, knowing that open importation would be prohibited.

'Again,' said Usher, 'the idea that someone would voluntarily carry such a huge mass of mouldering flesh and bone about, in hand luggage, was to my mind quite preposterous.'

Nevertheless, Cowman and Hodgson decided to check out this latest tale and travelled to Sri Lanka to interview the university authorities. They discovered that Perera had never been given a body for research, for export or otherwise.

'In many ways,' said Cowman, 'Sri Lankan society is living under Victorian standards, but their ledgers were a policeman's dream. Everything was written out in copperplate longhand.'

The two West Yorkshire policemen also met Nilanthe's grieving father, who confirmed that she had left for England with the Pereras and had never returned.

So what were Perera's motives for killing his adopted 'jungle girl'? Some sort of sex angle seemed likely, in view of Mrs Perera's earlier comments to the neighbours when Nilanthe first vanished. In any case, a jury at Leeds Crown Court found him guilty of unlawfully killing the girl, and on 11 March 1986 Dr Samuel Perera was gaoled for life.

In every way it had been a classic murder investigation, an immaculate piece of scientific and lay detection. Walter Cowman, who became head of Lincolnshire CID after the trial, commented: 'If Tom Hodgson had not been determined, had not refused to accept explanations which others may have accepted, who knows how things may have turned out?'

For Tom Hodgson, it set the seal on his police career. He retired soon afterwards. For Professor Usher the scientific side of the investigation was a personal triumph, but he is quick to point up Hodgson's part in the affair. 'To me, the abiding delight of the case was that this arrogant intellectual murderer obviously thought he was vastly superior to the hick Yorkshire copper who came to question him. But the final score was a resounding game, set and match to Tom.'

Right: *A team of experts spent several months reconstructing the victim's skeleton.*

Below: *The diagram shows which bones were found in Perera's laboratory and which in his house.*

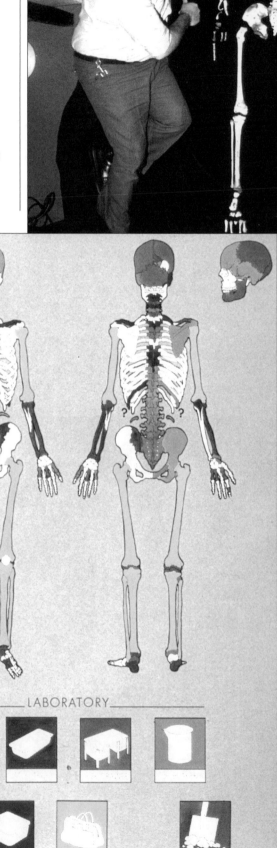

LABORATORY

122